HIS MYSTERIOUS WAYS

MIRACLES
OF HEALING

HIS MYSTERIOUS WAYS

MIRACLES
OF HEALING

FOREWORD BY EDWARD GRINNAN, EDITOR-IN-CHIEF, *GUIDEPOSTS*

Ideals Publications • Nashville, Tennessee

ISBN 0-8249-4610-3

Published by Ideals Publications, a division of Guideposts
535 Metroplex Drive, Suite 250
Nashville, Tennessee 37211
www.idealsbooks.com

Film separations by Precision Color Graphics, Franklin, Wisconsin
Printed and bound in the U.S.A. by Inland Press/Inland Book

Library of Congress CIP Data is on file.

Publisher, Patricia A. Pingry   Editor, Julie K. Hogan
Art Director, Eve DeGrie   Copy Editor, Lisa Ragan
Managing Editor, Peggy Schaefer   Editorial Assistant, Margaret A. Hogan

PHOTO CREDITS
Cover photo, Cape Cod National Seashore, © William H. Johnson; page 2, Glacier Bay National Park,
© Jeff Gnass; page 6, Bridger-Teton National Forest, © Carr Clifton; pages 9, 10, 17, 22, 26, 34, Mt.
Rainier, Washington, © Dennis Frates; pages 37, 38, 43, 51, 62, Summer Lake State Wildlife Refuge,
© Dennis Frates; pages 67, 68, 80, Alpine, Oregon, © Dennis Frates; pages 97, 98, 111, 120, 131,
Arches National Park, © William H. Johnson; pages 135, 136, 148, 154, 165, Klickitat County,
Washington, © Steve Terrill; pages 175, 176, 187, 198, Haystack Rock at Cape Kiwanda, Oregon,
© Steve Terrill.

Stories reprinted from *Guideposts* magazine, Carmel, NY 10512
Spot illustrations by Jo Anna Poehlmann

CONTENTS

FOREWORD — 7

HEAVEN SENT — 8

MYSTERIOUS HEALERS — 36

STRENGTH FROM SCRIPTURE — 66

TRUSTING GOD — 96

MIRACLES FROM PRAYER — 134

VISIONS OF ANGELS — 174

INDEX — 207

FOREWORD

We've all had them, those unexpected moments that make us stop and wonder, moments when we can't help but think, so this is how God is working in my life. In *Guideposts* magazine we call them "His Mysterious Ways," and for years these stories of divine coincidence have been the overwhelming favorite of our readers. In this special volume, we've collected the best of these stories—stories not just of miraculous physical healing but also spiritual healing. From ordinary people come these extraordinary accounts of lives touched by unforgettable grace—a family torn by strife mysteriously comes together again, a grieving widow receives an unmistakable sign of reassurance, a veteran finds freedom from guilt when talking to a fellow soldier.

All of us have times when an unseen hand brings us the comfort and hope we need to go on—powerful moments of mystery and grace when we meet the divine in our everyday lives.

Edward Grinnan
Editor-in-Chief, *Guideposts*

HEAVEN
SENT

All God's angels come to us disguised.

JAMES RUSSELL LOWELL

The Woman from Nowhere

LAURA Z. SOWERS, ALBUQUERQUE, NEW MEXICO

My preschooler son Marc and I were shopping in a large department store. On our way down to the main floor, Marc hopped on the escalator. I followed. Suddenly Marc screamed. I'd never heard a sound like that before. "Mama! My foot!"

Marc's right foot was wedged between the side of the moving step and the escalator's wall. His body was twisted toward me.

He screamed again. The escalator continued downward.

In the panic of the moment, the danger at the bottom of the escalator flashed before me—the thought of the foot being severed.

"Turn off the escalator!" I screamed. "Somebody, help!" And then, "Oh, dear God, dear God, help us! Help us!"

Several people at the base of the escalator began a flurry of activity. The escalator stopped! Someone had pressed an emergency button at the bottom of the steps.

"Thank You, Father," I prayed.

Marc clutched my arm and cried while I struggled to get a better look at his foot. A chill raced up my spine when I saw the tiny space in which his foot was trapped; it looked no more than a quarter of an inch wide. All I could see of his foot was his heel. The rest had disappeared into the jaws of the machine.

"Someone call the fire department!" I shouted.

Marc looked up at me desperately. "Mama," he said, "pray!"

I crouched next to him, holding him. I prayed. For a moment he quieted. Soon, though, he began crying again. "Daddy! Daddy!" he called out. I shouted out our business phone number, hoping someone would call my husband.

The two of us sat waiting. Marc cried. I patted his head. As the minutes passed I could see dark images of crutches and wheelchairs. I had always taken for granted that our little son would grow up playing baseball and soccer, running on strong legs and sturdy feet. Now, nothing seemed certain.

My prayers were as scattered as my feelings, and I searched my memory for a Bible verse to hold on to.

"And we know that all things work together for good to them that love God, to them who are the called according to his purpose" (Romans 8:28). This was one of the few verses I had memorized.

"You promised, Lord!" I cried. "And we know that all things . . ." Over and over I said that verse.

Marc looked up at me and said, "Mama, my bones feel broken and bleedy."

I clutched his blond head tighter to me, but now it was I who was feeling faint. "I can't faint, Lord," I prayed. "Marc needs me. O Lord, I know You're here." Where? "Help me."

At that moment I felt warm, soft arms enfolding me from

behind. A woman's soothing voice said quietly in my ear, "Jesus is here, Jesus is here."

The woman had come down the escalator and sat on the step above me. She gently rocked me from side to side, surrounding my shaking body with a calm embrace. "Tell your son his foot is all right," she said in my ear. There was an assurance in her voice.

"Marc," I said into his ear. "Your foot is all right."

"Tell him you'll buy him a new pair of shoes—whatever kind he wants."

"I'll buy you a new pair of shoes. Any kind you like."

Marc's crying stopped. "Cowboy boots? Like Daddy's?" We were talking about new shoes—new shoes for two healthy feet! For the first time since the ordeal began, I felt hope. Maybe, just maybe, his foot really would be all right.

"Tell him there are no broken bones," she said.

I did.

The firemen arrived. Two men with crowbars pried the step away from the escalator wall, freeing Marc's foot at last. His shoe was in tatters. It took all my courage to watch as the men pulled the shredded sock off Marc's foot, but when they did, they revealed a red, bruised, but whole foot.

I turned to share my joy with my wonderful friend, but all I saw was her leg as she turned the corner at the top of the escalator. I never even saw her face.

My husband, Craig, arrived just as the firemen were setting Marc down on the floor. He was still sobbing, but he could wiggle his toes. Later, x-rays confirmed what I already knew: no broken bones, only bruises and swelling.

To this day I do not know who the woman who helped me was, who knew that Jesus was there with us, who knew that the Lord keeps His promises.

Many people have suggested that the woman was an angel of the Lord. I can't be sure about that, but of this I am certain: She was heaven-sent.

*I couldn't work up the courage
to dial their number.*

CALLING THE IN-LAWS

ELISSA HADLEY CONKLIN, FISHKILL, NEW YORK

When my husband's father and his wife were visiting us over the summer, they got into a spat that dragged me in too. One remark led to another, and I found myself saying things I wished I hadn't. By the time my in-laws returned to Florida, they had patched things up, but I was on the outs with them.

I wanted to apologize, but instead of picking up the phone

I invariably put it off. They probably don't want to talk to me anyway, I rationalized. But the truth was I couldn't work up the courage to dial their number. Months went by and I did nothing except pray for guidance.

Then one day I was on the phone with a friend when a number flashed across my brand-new Caller ID screen. It was my in-laws! Was there something wrong? Was it an emergency?

I cut short my conversation and rang Florida the moment we hung up. My father-in-law answered.

"I'm so glad to talk to you," I blurted out at the sound of his voice. "I've been meaning to call and tell you how sorry I am for what happened." Soon we were laughing and joking, and then his wife got on. Apologies and explanations flew across the wires.

"Thanks for calling me," I finally said. "I just couldn't get up the nerve to contact you myself."

"What do you mean?" my father-in-law asked. "I didn't call. We just got in when the phone rang, and it was you."

I'd gotten Caller ID so I wouldn't miss important calls. I didn't know it would be used to help me make one.

AN UNLIKELY MEETING

JAN NOBLE, OAKTON, VIRGINIA

My husband, Rich, who'd been adopted as a baby, always brushed aside questions about whether he'd like to find his birth parents, saying, "If they didn't want me then, it's too late now." Still I knew that his stoic surface hid a deep ache. One night I noticed Rich crying at a television movie about a father and son. I decided to track down his birth family so he might find some closure.

All I had to go on was the information on Rich's birth certificate: his birthdate, October 16, 1941; his mother's name, Ruth Hicks Casselman; and her place of birth, Waupaca County, Wisconsin. I wrote to the hospital, went through old phone directories, searched the Internet—but no luck.

The only place left to try was the National Archives in Washington, D.C. One day in November 1999, I went to check the census records there. But I learned that by law, census information isn't released for seventy-two years. I was crushed. What good was such dated material?

I pulled the latest Waupaca census reel available—1920—from its file drawer. As I passed the first rows of microfilm readers, I overheard a man mention Wisconsin to the older woman with him. That's interesting, I thought before going on to my reader.

There was a listing for Hicks—Ruth! Encouraged, I went back for the 1910 reel. Maybe I could get names of relatives to follow up on. The slot where the reel should have been was empty. Then I remembered the folks I had overheard.

I walked over and peeked at their screen. Ruth Hicks,

Waupaca County, 1910! Amazed, I asked, "May I take a look when you're done? I'm trying to locate the family of Ruth Hicks . . ."

". . . Casselman?" the woman gasped. "She was my mother! Our family split up when I was little and I'm trying to find my baby brother. I've been looking for him for years."

Later that evening over dinner, the last chapter in the fam-ily history was finally closed. Shirley Casselman Garnett met her long-lost baby brother, my husband, Rich.

I saw a man thrashing in the water
next to me. In desperation,
I clutched to him.

PACIFIC OCEAN RESCUE

Donald Vairin, Oceanside, California

In July 1944, as a young hospital corpsman in the invasion of Guam, I huddled on the deck of the boat that would take me ashore with the troops. Our battleships lobbed shells to clear a path for us, and the Japanese fought back with everything they had. It was my first real action of the war. I was frightened.

Suddenly our boat came to a grinding halt. We'd hit a coral reef! "Everybody out!" the commanding officer barked.

I jumped into the ocean—and sank like a rock, my carbine rifle, medical pack, canteen and boots dragging me down. Determined to survive, I came up gasping for air, then sank again. I tried to pull off my boots, but the effort exhausted me. Finally, using the last of my strength, I struggled to the surface again.

I'm not going to make it! Then I saw a man thrashing in the water next to me. In desperation, I clutched to him. That was enough to hold me up and get me to the reef, where I was picked up by a boat headed back to the ship. I felt so guilty about grabbing the drowning man to save myself, I never told anyone about what had happened.

About six months later, on shore leave in San Francisco, I stopped in a restaurant. A sailor in uniform waved me over to sit with him and his friends. "This is my buddy," he announced. "He saved my life."

I recognized him as a member of our ship's crew, but I didn't know his name. I asked him what he was talking about.

"Don't you remember?" he said. "We were in the water together at Guam. You grabbed on to me. I was going down and you held me up."

HEARING RESTORED

CARLY DAWN ROGERS, BOISE, IDAHO

My older sister Tara and I were both diagnosed with hearing loss when we were children. Surgery helped me get some of my hearing back, but Tara lost all hers. I became my sister's ears. I learned sign language and everywhere we went I was her interpreter.

During the summer after my freshman year in high school, Tara and I attended our church's youth camp. We had to rough it: A four-mile hike in the middle of the night was one of the activities. It was a challenge to relay the guide's instructions to Tara by sign in the darkness. But it was all worth it, because we both looked forward to the popular inspirational speaker who was going to address us at the end of the week.

At sunset on our last day hundreds of us campers rushed toward the arena, jockeying for good seats. Tara and I ended up in the last row, where the sound from the PA system kept fading. I could barely hear the speaker. I glanced at Tara. Tears started to well in my eyes. *My sister will never know what this inspiring man has to say.*

23

I bowed my head. *God, we need you,* I prayed. I was at the edge of my seat trying to catch even one word. Then suddenly, incredibly, I could hear the speaker's voice loud and clear. I tapped Tara on the shoulder and began to sign furiously. But she stilled my hands and looked at me in amazement.

"Shh, Carly," she whispered. "I can hear him too."

*A 700-pound steel bracket
had fallen off the tractor and pinned
his father to the floor.*

HELP FROM A NEW FRIEND

PATRICIA WALWORTH WOOD, INDIANAPOLIS, INDIANA

Ten-year-old Billy Foy was busy with his homework in the family's mobile home outside of Albany, Indiana. His mother was at work and his father was out in the barn working on a tractor. Suddenly Duke, the mutt at Billy's side, began barking and jumping at the window.

"Calm down, Duke," Billy said. He looked to see if someone were outside or if a cat or a squirrel were racing up a tree.

Nothing. But Duke went on running from the window to the door. "Okay, okay," Billy said as he got up and let the dog out. There was something about the way Duke raced straight to the barn, barking all the way, that made Billy follow him.

In the barn Billy was shocked at what he found. A 700-pound steel bracket had fallen off the tractor and pinned his father to the floor.

Billy started to run back to the phone to call for help. "No," his father gasped, fighting for words, "get a jack."

Billy had worked with his father and knew how to operate the equipment. He used a hydraulic jack to raise the heavy bracket. Then with a floor jack he lifted the bracket enough for his father to roll out. "Thank God you came," Mr. Foy said to his son. "I was about to black out."

While recovering in the hospital, Billy Foy's father was told about what Duke had done. Mr. Foy had not wanted another dog and so Duke had been with them "on trial." He'd only been there three days.

He's been there ever since.

CALL ROY STANLEY

CHRISTINE SKILLERN, MUSCLE SHOALS, ALABAMA

It was almost dark when I went into the kitchen to fix some supper. I didn't feel a bit hungry, but there are two rules we insulin-dependent diabetics must adhere to: take insulin regularly and don't skip meals.

So I shook some oatmeal into a pan of water and set it to cooking on a front burner of my electric stove. I started across the kitchen to get milk from the refrigerator, but I never made it. My feet slipped out from under me and I fell hard, flat on my back, on the floor.

Oh, you've done it now, old girl.

I pushed and stretched and made every effort to get up, but I couldn't even sit up. Nothing I could do was going to get this overweight, seventy-year-old body off the floor. I needed help. I thought about screaming, but who would hear me? I was a widow who lived alone and had already closed and locked all the windows and doors.

The telephone! I could call my sister, Martha. The telephone hung high on the wall, over near my bedroom door. Next to it was my broom, propped against the wall.

I dug my elbows into the rough texture of the floor covering and managed to slide on my back a couple of inches. Six or seven more shoves and a lot of panting put me near the phone. Using the broom, I gave it a whack that sent the handset banging to the floor. But to my dismay, I couldn't make a call. The dial was up on the phone.

Fear was beginning to gnaw at me. The burner under my oatmeal was glowing brightly. What would happen if the water boiled out? Would the metal pan melt and ruin my stove? Would it set my house on fire?

But there was nothing I could do. I was locked in my house with no way to contact the outside world and no light except the glow from the electric burner.

Finally I whispered, "Lord Jesus, I'm so alone and I'm afraid. Please come and be here with me. Quiet me, Jesus, and protect me, and please take care of my pan of oatmeal."

The air began to chill as the evening grew longer. I hugged my arms about me and wished for a blanket. I dragged myself into the bedroom and looked longingly at the heavy spread on my bed. I could never pull that down. But there were some clothes lying on the cedar chest. Again I dug my elbows into the rug, and I pulled down a sweater and skirt to cover myself.

As the night grew blacker, I thought of the insulin shot I normally took after supper. What condition would I be in by morning? Was I going to die? My back was beginning to ache. I had no idea what damage I had done to myself. Panic began to smother me.

"Lord," I prayed, "don't leave me. Please stay with me and

comfort me." Then I began to recite Scripture verses, mostly those I'd learned in Sunday school, one verse after another, until I slipped into a fitful sleep.

When the light of morning roused me, I thanked God that the long night was over and my house was not burned.

I said my morning prayers and made another attempt to get up from the floor. I could not move. My throat was dry and I was hungry. And how long could I go without insulin?

Surely a neighbor would telephone. Oh, no! The phone was off the hook. But then, maybe someone would come and knock on the door.

All morning I listened carefully but no knock came. I kept praying, "Jesus, please help me."

Around noon a thought flashed through my mind: *Call someone.*

Another thought: *Call your friends.*

"But the phone . . ." I said aloud.

I began to call out names. I started with my sister; I knew she'd be at work. Then I called my neighbors, one by one, pausing after each, listening for a knock.

I had run out of names to call when another sudden thought invaded my tired mind: *Call Roy Stanley.* Roy had stopped by two days earlier to pray with me, but he lived so far away.

Still the thought persisted: *Call Roy.*

So I began calling, "Roy, please come to me. I need you." I said it aloud, over and over without stopping.

It was about two o'clock when I heard a loud knocking on the back door. I yelled, "Come and help me! I need you!"

Then I heard a series of heavy blows and a splintering of wood. Footsteps . . . and Roy was standing over me.

"Christine!" he exclaimed. "What are you doing on the floor?"

I told him.

Roy went to the kitchen to get some water for my parched throat. He phoned my sister and called for an ambulance. Then as we waited he told me how he happened to be there.

Roy and his wife were at home when he felt a strong urge to check on me. He told his wife, "I have to go to Christine. Something has happened to her."

When he knocked on my door, he got no answer, but something seemed to urge him: *Don't leave. Go to the back and knock again.* So he went around to the back door, knocked harder, and finally heard me calling, "Come and help me! I need you!"

As the ambulance arrived, I felt a strange sense of elation. Jesus had been with me through the night. He'd brought Roy to rescue me. He'd answered every single one of my prayers, even the one about the oatmeal. For when I finally thought about that burner, I said to Roy, "Will you please check on a pan of oatmeal I put on to cook last night? It must be burned black by now."

A strange expression crossed Roy's face. "I turned that burner off when I got the water for you," he said. "Did you say you put it on last night? Christine, that oatmeal is not burned. In fact, it's just ready to eat now!"

*I tried to draw in deep breaths
but could only manage shallow gasps.
My lungs were screaming for oxygen.*

THE FLUTTER OF TINY WINGS

JANELLE RICE, POLLOCK PINES, CALIFORNIA

Because of lung problems, I need supplemental oxygen all the time. A device in my bathroom pumps extra oxygen into my bedroom. By using a hose extension I can move safely around the house or even work in my garden.

One night I awoke at about 4:00 A.M., my throat bone-dry. I needed a drink of water. Thinking I could make it without the oxygen hose, I headed the short distance to the bathroom.

As I filled a glass, I found myself struggling to breathe. The heat given off by the pump made the air warm and stale. I tried to draw in deep breaths but could only manage shallow gasps. My lungs were screaming for oxygen.

I sank onto the edge of the tub. I knew I needed to get out of there, but I was too weak. God, please help me!

Suddenly, close to the right side of my head I felt a vibration, like the rapid fluttering of tiny wings. It seemed as though invisible fans stirred the heavy air; a cool, almost imperceptible current flowed across my mouth and nose. The slight movement of air was enough to relax my breathing. Gradually my gasps became less frantic, and I was able to make my way shakily back to the bedroom.

There was no possible source for the current of air in the bathroom. But it was unmistakably there, accompanied by the faint reassuring flutter of tiny wings. The Bible says, "He shall give his angels charge over thee." That doesn't necessarily mean big, stately angels. Small ones will do.

An Unexpected Garden

Billie F. Harvey, Central, South Carolina

It was a warm November day when I carried the basket of jonquil bulbs out to the yard. I should have planted them the previous fall, but before I could our son was killed in a car accident. As a year of grief passed, they lay forgotten in a basket. Now, having discovered the bulbs again, I tried to stir up some enthusiasm to plant them.

I kneeled down in the yard and stuck the spade into the

moist reddish soil. I dug a hole and planted a bulb, dug a hole and planted another. Since Eddie had died, all the activities in my life seemed like chores. I covered a bulb with dirt and reached into the basket for another. Deep down I didn't believe anything would ever ease my pain.

Suddenly, the bulb in my hand crumbled and fell apart. "Dead!" I cried out to nobody. "They're dead!" I snatched the remaining bulbs and despondently crushed them in my hands, dashing the pieces to the wind.

Winter passed, and then one early spring morning I glanced out at the yard from a window. I couldn't believe my eyes. I rushed outside for a closer look. There at my feet bright-yellow jonquils bloomed! In each spot where I had planted a "dead" bulb, strong and healthy flowers grew.

I stood still before this unexpected garden. And clearly, as if spoken aloud, I heard the promise, "I am the resurrection, and the life: he that believeth in me, though he were dead, yet shall he live."

Now, each spring when the jonquils bloom, I remember, and I answer, "Yes, Lord, I believe."

MYSTERIOUS
HEALERS

Messengers from God take many surprising forms.

AUTHOR UNKNOWN

RESCUED FROM A BEE STING

PEARL MAURER, ST. GEORGE, UTAH

I was gardening one afternoon at our summer cottage on Lake Ontario. I'd grabbed a clump of weeds near an old tree trunk when I suddenly recoiled. Too late. Out swarmed a squad of angry bees. I got a nasty sting on my hand—I had forgotten my gloves.

I yanked out the stinger and rushed toward the cottage for ice, but I didn't get far. Nausea and dizziness swept over me, then I had trouble breathing. I'm having a reaction. I've got to get help. My husband was working and the kids were in town with their friends. I glanced across the yard to see if my neighbor Donna was around. No car in the driveway, no sign of anyone home.

My whole arm was swelling now and my joints ached. Only a rising sense of panic kept me moving. Maybe Donna's parents are home. Their cottage was right behind Donna's. I staggered out of the yard, past two driveways. I'm not going to make it. I tried to shout. No words came out. I made it to the porch steps, praying, Somebody be home. Please hear me!

The last thing I remember was reaching for the doorbell.

When I came to, people were hovering around me. "She's DOA," one said. No, I'm not! I thought before slipping back into unconsciousness.

I awoke in a hospital bed with a doctor standing over me. He looked relieved. I glanced around the room. There were Donna, my husband, and the kids.

"Good thing you got here when you did, Mrs. Maurer," the doctor said. "Another few minutes and you wouldn't have survived that allergic reaction to the bee sting. You went into anaphylactic shock."

The doctors kept me overnight for observation. In the morning, Donna came by to fill in the gaps in my memory. "You rang my parents' bell and then collapsed. They told me they heard the bell and came running."

"Thank God they did!"

"That's the odd part. They're both almost completely deaf. They haven't been able to hear that doorbell in years."

When the results of my biopsy came in,
the doctor informed me J had
a cancerous tumor.

S EARCH FOR A S URGEON

A NNE A BRUZZINI , T URLOCK , C ALIFORNIA

The dream was so vivid and unusual I told my husband about it as soon as I awoke. "I was explaining to a woman with shoulder-length, golden-brown hair and a white lab coat that I felt a pain in my left breast," I said. "But I've never noticed anything like that."

"You should see your gynecologist, just in case," he said. I did and, to my shock, there was a lump in my breast. When the results of my biopsy came in, the doctor informed me I had a cancerous tumor. He wanted to perform a mastectomy.

"Couldn't you do a more conservative surgery," I asked, "take out just the lump?"

"No," he replied. "A mastectomy is the best course of treatment."

"I'd like a second opinion," I said.

A friend then gave me the name of her oncologist. Before my appointment, I read up on breast cancer so I'd be able to make a more informed decision about treatment. The most important thing, though, would be finding a doctor I could trust. Lord, I asked, how will I know who's the right one for me?

My friend's oncologist put me at ease right away and I told him I wanted to avoid losing my breast, if at all possible. "I'd like you to see this surgeon I work with," he said, then set up an appointment for me.

I drove straight over. The moment I saw the surgeon, I knew that I'd finally found my doctor. Standing there in her white lab coat, her honey-colored hair falling around her shoulders, was the woman I'd seen in my dream.

THE BOOK LADY

TERRY A. ZIER, TUMWATER, WASHINGTON

Plumping up the pillow beneath my head, I sighed and stared at the ceiling. Fine cracks spread like wispy spider webs across the white expanse. The room was silent but for my breathing. I turned my head toward the door. No one would venture down this deserted hospital hallway. Except for my parents, I hadn't any visitors since being admitted because my doctor did not yet know what was wrong with me. I had been far too tired for a normal thirteen-year-old and was having trouble digesting my food. Some days I was almost too weak to walk, but there seemed to be no medical explanation for my condition.

Tears stung my eyes. I was tired of having no one to talk to. A roommate was out of the question. The quarantine sign on my door meant even the nuns steered clear. What can I do stuck alone in this room? Then a knock came at the door.

It swung open and a woman stepped in, pulling a cart behind her. Her uniform told me she was a candy striper, but she was middle-aged, not a teenager. She smiled at me warmly, and I found myself smiling back. She wasn't too tall, and she had light brown hair. "Call me the book lady," she announced, coming right up to my bed and holding out her hand. I started. Hadn't she seen the sign on my door?

"It's all right," she said, "I understand." She patted my shoulder. "Now, let's see what goodies we have in here." She turned to her cart. I could feel a lump rising in my throat. I was not a great reader.

"Here," she said, handing me a slim hardcover. "What about *Rebecca of Sunnybrook Farm*?" I bit my lip. "What's wrong?" the lady asked. "It's hard for me to read," I admitted, shame turning my stomach to jelly. The book lady sat at the edge of my bed. "What better time to improve your reading than now?" she asked. "Are you scared?" I nodded. "That's okay. Everybody gets scared sometimes."

"The doctor doesn't know what's wrong with me," I said, fiddling with the bedspread. "And nobody visits me because I might make them sick. I wish I had someone to talk to."

The book lady tilted her head and looked at me. "You can always talk to God. He wants you to. And He always listens. That's why He's there." I had never really heard much about God before. "He'll listen to me when I'm sad?" I asked, wanting to make sure. Maybe I didn't have to feel so lonely. "Of course," the book lady said. "Especially when you're sad." She rose and straightened her red-and-white-striped smock. "I'll come by day after tomorrow," she promised. "So start reading *Rebecca* and we'll talk about it then." Flashing me another dazzling smile, she gripped the handle of her cart and started out of my room.

"What's your name?" I asked. She stopped for a minute and

looked at me kindly. "Like I said, you can call me the book lady. Bye-bye." I waved, and then she and her cart were gone. I fingered the frayed binding of *Rebecca*. The book lady was right. This was the perfect time to work on my reading. Flipping to the first page, I began the first chapter.

Two days later, as promised, the book lady came back.

"How are you liking the story?" she asked, coming close to me as she had the first time. "Very much, thank you," I said, suddenly shy. "I've been reading a lot." Fluffing her bobbed hair, the lady nodded. "That's good." She held out another book. "It's the next in the collection. I think you'll really enjoy it." A shiver of anticipation ran through me when I took the next *Rebecca* book in my hands. "Thank you," I replied, lying back on my pillow. "Rest now," the lady said. "I'll see you day after tomorrow."

All that day and the next I read my books and talked to God. "Thank you for sending me a friend," I said. "And please help the doctor find out what's wrong with me so I can go home soon." I felt a lot better when I talked to God.

Every other morning for a month and a half the lady visited

me, introducing me to countless friends in the books she brought.

Then one morning, after the nurse had taken my breakfast tray, my doctor came in. "Terry," he said, "we're sending you home this morning. Whatever was ailing you seems to have gone away."

Home! The doctor said my father was waiting for me in the lobby. I dressed and went down with the nurse in the elevator. "How are you, Missy?" Dad asked.

"Glad to be leaving the hospital!" I said, grinning. He took my hand.

"Wait!" I had almost forgotten my friend. "I want to say good-bye to the book lady." The nurse looked at me curiously. "Is she working today?" I asked.

"What book lady?" my doctor wondered.

"The book lady," I insisted. "In a candy-striper uniform. She came by my room every other day while I was here."

The nurse shook her head. "We haven't had a book volunteer for a long, long time," she said. "And I'm afraid this hospital doesn't use candy stripers."

"But she visited me. . . . " my voice trailed off. The doctor and nurse eyed me suspiciously, as if worried they'd released me too soon.

"Come on, Missy," my dad said. "Let's go."

"Bye, now," called the nurse. "Take care," called the doctor. Dad and I walked out into the sun toward the car. I knew there had been a book lady, no matter what anybody said. She might not have worked for the hospital. But she did work for God. "Can we stop at the library?" I asked my father. "I have some new friends waiting there."

At the hospital a neurosurgeon
and a plastic surgeon examined John
while I paced outside the treatment room.

THE THIRD DOCTOR

SUE MCCUSKER, CANTON, GEORGIA

The first thing I noticed that morning in my fiancé's hospital room was the chair close to his bed. That's odd, I thought. I knew the chair hadn't been there when I had left well after the end of visiting hours the night before.

Twenty-four hours earlier it had been a beautiful, sunny day when John and I went for a long bike ride. John had lost control on a rough patch of road and fallen hard onto the asphalt. At the hospital a neurosurgeon and a plastic surgeon examined John while I paced outside the treatment room.

Finally the doctors let me in to see him. John looked weak and pallid.

"He has a bad concussion," one of the specialists told me.

"There's nothing more we can do right now," said the second. "Go home and try to get some sleep."

I sat by John's side for a few hours. Then, before I left, I prayed, "Dear Lord, please watch over him tonight."

This morning John looked so much better; the color had come back to his face and he seemed more relaxed. As I stood by his bed, he woke up, smiling, alert. We talked about the accident.

"Thank goodness for those three doctors," he said.

"Three?" I wondered aloud.

"Yes, there was a doctor with a beard who watched over me all night. He sat right in that chair."

I looked at the chair. And I knew my prayer had been answered.

RISE UP AND WALK

JOAN B. PARIS, PEACHTREE CITY, GEORGIA

After my grandfather died, my uncle Bill was the only one left living in the old family home with my grandmother. She was ninety-three and he was sixty-five, but they depended on each other like siblings. He'd get the Nashville newspaper every morning and bring her breakfast and keep her up-to-date on the rest of the family.

One morning, though, after twenty-three years of the same

routine, he got up at seven o'clock, swung both feet over the side of his bed and suddenly collapsed to the floor with a stroke. Conscious but unable to move, he yelled to my grandmother in her bedroom, "Mama, Mama!"

"Why are you hollering so early in the morning?" she called back, roused from her sleep.

"Mama," he said, "come quick."

Grandmother knew then that something was terribly wrong. Quickly she called to the One Who had never failed to hear her every prayer, then got out of bed. She hurried to my uncle's room, where he lay paralyzed. Knowing help was needed, she telephoned their next-door neighbor and went downstairs to let the neighbor in. Together they went to Bill's room; medical help was summoned and soon arrived.

What was so unusual about this? Wouldn't any mother have done the same? Yes, perhaps. But you see, Grandmother had been permanently injured in a car accident and since then had fallen, breaking her hip twice. She had been in a wheelchair for nine years. During that time she had not taken one step by herself.

*As the performance day grew closer,
Dad's swollen leg became discolored. Our
thoughts of gangrene, and of amputation,
didn't seem so far-fetched.*

53

VISIT TO A FLOWER SHOP

HELEN HASAPES, TARZANA, CALIFORNIA

About two weeks before my dad, age seventy-two and founder of the Samson Seventies Strongmen, was to present an exhibition at the Motion Picture and Television Home for retired show biz folks, he slipped off a ladder and injured his leg. He had been pruning trees in his Woodland Hills yard. Fortunately, the fall wasn't from a great height; the problems were caused by the way he landed.

My older sister, Cathy, and I rushed him to the doctor, who prescribed large doses of ibuprofen as a painkiller and anti-inflammatory. When I stopped by to see Dad a couple of days later, I expected him to be up, working around the house or heading for the gym as always. Instead, he was in bed, and his injured left leg was swollen to twice its normal size.

"The doctor says it's lymphatic fluid," he said. "He wants to see me again in a few days if the swelling hasn't gone down." The specter of a family friend who had recently lost a limb to gangrene came into my mind, as I'm sure it had come into Dad's.

"So what's the worst that can happen?" he asked. "They'll give me a peg leg and I'll become a pirate!" And he launched into a medley from *The Pirates of Penzance*.

Upbeat as he tried to be, I could tell he was worried. What could I do? All my life, Dad had been there for me. My mother had died young, leaving him with two toddler girls. Various aunts and my grandmother had offered to raise us, but Dad had promised Mom he would take care of us no matter what, and he did.

Born in Alliance, Ohio, Theo Hasapes was the son of a

Greek circus strongman. Dad wasn't a tall boy, but he was sturdy. At Indiana University, he lettered in three sports. There's even an old newspaper photo of left-end Theodore Hasapes running downfield, carrying another player above his head.

Dad stayed with sports, becoming a high school coach in California. He was a doting father, sharing his indomitable spirit—and his Christian faith—with Cathy and me. A down-to-earth man, he never lost his sense of awe before the majesty of God or before the protection God sends in the form of people and of angels.

His faith was the basis of his sense of adventure, his love of fun and his devotion to a healthy body. Even in his fifties, he worked out in the gym five days a week, exercising and weight training.

"Dad, you should start a club," Cathy and I teased, "for other men who are fifty and fit!" Dad laughed and said, "Someday."

Years later, when he turned sixty-nine, he said, "I've been thinking. Maybe a club wouldn't be such a bad idea after all."

Instead of Fit and Fifty, the club became the Samson

Seventies Strongmen—seventy being the minimum age for membership. It was formed to encourage seniors to exercise. Its philosophy: Age is no barrier to good health and physical fitness.

The club took off. The men who joined early on were already in shape and enjoyed working out together. As news of their presentations spread, they were invited to perform all over California. Usually five members went to a performance. Each demonstrated a feat of strength with weights, then talked a bit about himself. Quiet and unassuming in private, Dad came alive in front of an audience. And the audiences—especially seniors— loved him.

The performance for the Motion Picture and Television Home in Calabasas was going to be a highlight of the club's year. Since Dad was from a family of performers himself, he really looked forward to the club doing a vaudeville-style show for retirees "in the biz."

Yet, as the performance day grew closer, Dad's swollen leg became discolored. Our thoughts of gangrene, and of amputation, didn't seem so far-fetched.

A week after Dad's accident, I drove down Ventura

Boulevard to open the florist shop my sister and I owned in Encino. As I drove, my emotions spun out of control. I blamed myself for Dad's accident. If only I had encouraged him to retire to a rocker instead of an active lifestyle! Then I blamed God. Couldn't He have kept Dad safely on a ladder?

I pulled into a parking space and killed the engine. I sat for a minute, getting hold of myself. I knew the next step was to take Dad to the emergency room. He was in so much pain, I thought he was about ready to give in and go.

Inside the shop, I looked over the day's orders and began arranging a floral bouquet. The tears that had been trickling down my face gave way to quiet sobs. Time stopped. I felt a moment of profound silence—then a rush of cool air. I looked up and saw a woman. She was surrounded by a blur of bright light. I had to blink before I could see her clearly. That's odd, I thought. I didn't hear the bell or the door opening.

I shook my head, unobtrusively, I hoped, and smiled at her. Now everything seemed normal. She was dressed in a long white skirt and a blue blouse trimmed with white lace. I guessed her to be in her thirties. Brown hair fell below her slim shoulders.

"Why are you crying, my dear?" she asked in a soft, motherly voice.

I brushed away tears with the backs of my hands and said, "I'll be okay. How can I help you, ma'am?"

"Perhaps I can help you," she said.

Overcome, I began pouring out the story of my family, about the mother I couldn't remember, her death, Dad's devotion. I could feel the woman's gaze as I explained what had happened to Dad, his leg filling up with fluid and not responding to medication, and all my worry and guilt.

She listened intently, never taking her eyes off me. Simply being in her presence brought a calm, peaceful reassurance; the pressure and fear began to dissipate. When I finished my story, instead of offering sympathy, she began to explain, step-by-step, what I needed to do to save my father's leg. She clearly and precisely listed the items I would need and how to use them.

I never questioned her authority; it was clear she knew exactly what she was talking about. She even knew the layout of Dad's living room!

Then, placing her hand ever so softly on my shoulder, she

said, "Have no fear, my dear. The hand of God guides you always. Pray; have faith. Your father's leg will heal."

Motioning for her to wait, I entered the walk-in refrigerator and brought out a bouquet of long-stemmed red roses and ferns to thank her. When I returned she was gone. I hurried out the front door, but she was nowhere to be seen, not on the sidewalk or in neighboring stores. Why had she come into a florist shop if she hadn't wanted flowers?

I hurriedly turned the sign on the door to "Closed." As I rushed out, the phone on the counter began to ring, but I kept going.

First I stopped at my house in Tarzana to pick up the necessary items. Then I quickly headed west for Woodland Hills, where Dad lived. Traffic on the 134 was snarled, yet I felt relaxed and energetic, even optimistic.

I greeted Dad with my usual kiss. He looked downhearted and glanced nervously at his leg, which had taken on a bluish-purple discoloration. "I called the flower shop," he said. "Nobody answered. It hurts too much for me to drive myself to the hospital. In fact, I can barely walk."

Wasting no time, I took the items from my bag and placed them on the coffee table next to the couch where Dad lay. When he saw the rope I use for a clothesline, he looked confused.

"Is this some sort of joke, Helen?"

"No, Dad. Now, please listen. We've got no time to lose, and I'm going to need your cooperation. If it doesn't work, I'll drive you straight to the hospital. In the meantime, we're going to do exactly what the lady in the shop told me to do."

Dad raised a questioning eyebrow. "This lady—was she a doctor?"

"No, Dad," I said with a confident smile as I carefully measured a length of rope. "Does she really have to be?"

First, I made a loop with one end of the rope, then tied the other around the low-hanging beam directly above Dad's couch. Next I folded a small towel and placed it over the rope-loop to cushion the weight of his leg. With Dad flat on his back, I gently raised his swollen leg and placed it into the hanging loop. Then I began rubbing olive oil over his calf and the area above his knee. "Is that all?" he asked, a little surprised.

"It wouldn't hurt to pray," I said.

Using two hands, I continued a massaging motion upwards. While I concentrated on the calf, Dad worked the area above his knee. And then, for a moment, I thought I felt a movement in the lymphatic fluid! Was it my imagination? Then Dad broke into a winning smile. He felt it too.

By the next morning, Dad was no longer in danger. The stagnant lymphatic fluid was drained back into the venous system and had circulated out of the affected limb. The swelling was gone. There would be no peg-legged pirates in our family.

Dad was back at the gym six days later, getting in shape for the residents of the Motion Picture and Television Home. The performance was a huge success, and the feats of strength drew oohs and aahs from the audience. But the most amazing feat had come earlier in the week when a stranger entered our florist shop to deliver the greatest strength of all—God's healing power.

MESSAGE FROM A FRIEND

JILL RENICH-MEYERS, MECHANICSBURG, PENNSYLVANIA

My husband, Fred, passed away suddenly. I was grief-stricken. I prayed for something—anything—to hang on to. One dark day I felt especially alone. I walked out to get the mail, opened the box and found a card from my friend Elizabeth. She had lost her husband six months earlier.

How is she managing? I wondered as I ripped open the envelope. Inside the card, across from the printed message, she had written in ink in her distinctive hand, "It does get easier." Her words lessened my despair a little. God, if your healing is there for Elizabeth, it must be there for me too.

To try to get my mind off things I started cleaning the house. While dusting behind Fred's desk I found the shoes he had bought the week before he died. Fred will never walk with me again, I thought, tears forming in my eyes. Then, softly, Elizabeth's message came to mind. I opened her card. It does get easier. I wiped away my tears and continued my chores.

During the next several months—with the help of family, friends, and prayer—things did get easier. But nothing meant more to me than Elizabeth's words.

Months later I took out Elizabeth's card again. I wanted to drop her a line. When I opened the card I couldn't believe my eyes. There was no handwritten message. No personal writing at all except for her signature. God had transferred His comforting words from her card to my heart.

I was suffering one of my worst asthma attacks. . . . I was wheezing and gasping for breath.

SOMEONE AT MY SIDE

BARRY RUDESILL, MONTELLO, WISCONSIN

The Lord sustains him on his sickbed . . ." (Psalm 41:3, RSV) I was suffering one of my worst asthma attacks. It was so bad that Mom took me to the hospital, where a doctor gave me a shot. "This is about the best we can do for you," he said. "If you're having problems in the morning, come back immediately."

That night I asked my parents to set up a bed for me on the living room couch. I didn't want to keep my brother up; I was wheezing and gasping for breath.

For a long while I tossed and turned. I didn't have the strength to get out of bed, so I lay there, listening to the sounds of the night, praying for relief. At last a time came when my breathing eased and I drifted off to sleep.

When I woke up, Mom was leaning over me, smiling. "Barry, how do you feel?"

"Fine," I said, breathing deeply. "No problem." Then I noticed a chair that had been pulled close to the couch as if someone had been sitting there. "Did you or Dad come in after I went to sleep?" I asked.

"No," Mom said, "we listened, but you seemed to be getting better."

"But when did you move the chair next to me?"

"Why, Barry," she said, "we didn't."

"I didn't either!" I exclaimed. "I couldn't have moved last night if I had tried."

And then I remembered the feeling I'd had as I dozed off. Someone—yes, Someone— was sitting at my side.

STRENGTH
FROM SCRIPTURE

Heal me, O Lord, and I shall be healed.

JEREMIAH 17:14A

Heal Me, O Lord

MARILYN LUDOLF, WINSTON-SALEM, NORTH CAROLINA

I woke up with the same tormenting headache I had gone to bed with and struggled to the bathroom. I grasped the sink with both hands and reluctantly raised my pounding head to the mirror. The face reflected in the glass was a fiery red mask of tiny bumps and large acne-like sores. Hundreds of them. The horrible rash covered my face like the Egyptian plague of boils in the Bible. The unending headache and rash comprised the mysterious condition I had lived with for twelve long, unbearable years. Here I was, a middle-aged woman with two teenage sons and a husband, and I could hardly bear to raise my head and look in the mirror.

Tears blurred my vision as I tried to remember the smooth, milk-white complexion I used to have. My fingers twitched, longing to claw at the fiercely itching skin on my face.

I had tried everything—special diets, oatmeal soap, baby oil, vitamins and enough creams and ointments to fill a small drugstore. And the long line of doctors I had seen had passed by like a dwindling parade of hope. The rash had only grown worse, and my face swelled, itched and turned tomato-red at the slightest stimulus.

Suddenly the pain behind my eyes tightened as if someone were packing cotton into my sinuses. I reached for a bottle of pain medication and quickly swallowed a couple of pills. I took the maximum of eight pills a day. But they only forestalled the worst of it—when the pain crept down my neck, making clear thinking nearly impossible.

I felt consumed by despair, by the long years of this strange affliction. I had prayed so many times for it to go away. "Oh, God, why don't you help me?"

I dabbed at my eyes and dressed for work. My head ached so much I could hardly pull a comb through my hair. I thought about crawling back into bed. But, of course, I couldn't. I liked my work as a third grade schoolteacher. I had to keep going.

As I entered school that morning a little girl peered up at me, her eyes wide with surprise and dismay. "How come your face looks like that?" she asked.

I raised my hands over my cheeks and tried to explain. But I fell silent. I had no answer.

Not long after, someone told me about a dermatologist. I had seen half a dozen specialists already, but I made an appointment, ready to grasp at anything. I sat slumped on his examining table after a long series of allergy tests.

"Well, maybe we have an answer," the doctor said. "It appears you are allergic to yourself."

I stared at him in disbelief. "You must be kidding!"

"I know it sounds strange, but these allergy tests show you are allergic to your own bacteria."

Hope blew away like the last autumn leaf. Allergic to myself. How could I escape that?

"We'll make a special serum, using your saliva," said the doctor, "and teach you how to inject it."

And so began the next three years of giving myself shots. The headaches were not quite as severe, nor the rash quite as red—partial relief. The doctor did everything he could, prescribing medicines, creams, and consultations. Still, the ever-present plague was agonizing, embarrassing.

So I followed my old, exhausted pattern and found yet another doctor. This time an outstanding allergist. More tests. More money. He decided I was allergic to a long list of foods, and put me on a diet. For a year I existed on nothing but peas, potatoes, carrots, lettuce and lean meat. My weight plummeted to 102 pounds.

"You're wasting away, Mama," said my son one morning as I packed my lunch of canned peas. He was right. Something dreadful was happening to me. And despite it all the daily headaches persisted and the humiliating rash and acne were splashed across my face as big and red as ever.

This is no way to live, I thought dismally as I draped a scarf across my head and left for work.

Then one Sunday as I struggled to teach my Sunday school class, I heard myself saying, "God is the answer." I paused, the echo of my words thundering in my head. As the class continued, the words burrowed inside me like a splinter.

At home after church I lay on the sofa with a warm cloth across my forehead. I gazed out the windows at the silent woods across the road. The words I had spoken that morning nudged at me. I am a Christian, I thought. I tell other people God is the answer, that they can find wholeness through Him. Yet I've been a prisoner of this condition for nearly sixteen years.

Suddenly the familiar story of the woman in Mark 5:25–34 focused in my mind: The woman who touched the hem of Jesus' robe and was healed. I was so much like her. I too had suffered a condition for many years, gone to countless physicians, spent nearly all I had and was not better but worse. The difference was the woman in Mark had finally gone to Jesus with faith—and was healed.

Did such healings still happen today? I wondered. If so,

could healing really happen to me? There on the sofa, the idea of real healing from God spun in my head. It almost seemed too ancient to be real. If only I could be sure.

The weeks passed and winter melted away. The incredible idea of healing lingered in my mind like a held-over Christmas present. I toyed with the ribbons, afraid to open it, afraid it might turn out to be empty . . . but strangely unable to turn away.

Then one Sunday something happened. I lay in bed trying to find diversion from my headache by watching television. On the screen stood a beautiful young woman—Cheryl Prewitt, Miss America 1980.

"God healed me," she said. "I prepared myself to be healed, and God healed me."

My heart began to pound with a strange excitement. She was speaking to me! No, God was speaking to me! He did still heal people today.

"Come quick!" I called to my husband and boys. As they hurried to the bedroom, I pointed to the TV, where the radiant young woman still spoke. Tears poured down my face. "If God can heal her, then He can heal me," I said.

73

Finally, after sixteen desperate years of trying everything else, I was ready. Again I relived that Biblical story in my mind. What was it Jesus had said to that woman after she had brushed her fingertips across His robe? "Your faith has made you whole." And what had Cheryl Prewitt said? "I prepared myself to be healed."

Faith, that was the key. That was what had been missing before. My faith had grown flabby, like out-of-shape muscles. I knew intellectually that God is powerful and can heal. But somehow I had to get that knowledge from my mind down into my heart. I had to believe it as absolutely as I believed the sun would rise tomorrow.

On May 1, I began to prepare myself for healing like an athlete training for the Olympics. I sat down in the kitchen rocker with a pad of paper and my Bible. I flipped to the concordance in the back—to the heading of "healing, health, and faith." I picked out verses, then looked them up, writing each one down word for word. It took a couple of days, but I finally compiled a list of thirty-six Scriptures—sort of a training manual for my faith.

The next day I tucked the papers into my purse. While driving to work I pulled them out and laid them on the seat. At the first stoplight I focused on Psalm 103:2-3. "Bless the Lord, O my soul, and forget not all his benefits . . . who healeth all thy diseases," I whispered. I closed my eyes, saying it over and over, letting it sink down inside me. At a stop sign my eyes fell on another: "Heal me, O Lord, and I shall be healed. . . ." (Jeremiah 17:14). I said it over and over.

All day I kept it up—before getting out of the car, walking along the school corridors, sitting in the playground at recess. Not a spare moment was lost; by the end of the school day my Scripture papers were dog-eared from wear.

In the weeks that followed, this became my constant routine. The papers were as inseparable from me as my shadow. And by some inexplicable process, the thirty-six Scriptures were slowly sinking into the core of my being with roots of belief. I was actually beginning to believe—really believe—that I could be healed. I could almost feel my faith stretching and rippling with new strength.

I circled the twelfth of July on the kitchen calendar. "Lord, this is the day I'm asking for complete healing," I said.

Then I added another exercise. I began to visualize my complexion as pink and clear as a newborn baby's, and my sinus passages free and well. I imprinted it on my mind day and night. This exercise became rather a strenuous one, because the mirror was such a contrast from my image. The mirror is wrong, I told myself. Soon it will reflect my inner image.

Late that spring I hurried past a mirror at school. Suddenly I stopped, backed up, and peered into it. I ran my fingers across my face. Was it my imagination or did the fiery-red rash seem a bit faded? And my headache. Didn't it seem better? "Oh, thank you, Lord!" I cried. "You are healing me."

July 12 dawned warm and shiny through the bedroom window. I tiptoed to the bathroom mirror, took a deep breath, and looked into it. The rash still lingered on the lower part of my face, and a faint sinus headache tugged behind my eyes. I will not give up, I thought. With a sudden burst of faith I said, "Well, Lord, this is the day! I know it will happen."

When the sun set in an orange glow I went to a mirror again. Again I stared at my reflection, tears sparkling on my face.

A face completely smooth and clear! It was the face I had imagined. The headache of the morning had drifted away as well. God and faith had made me whole.

For almost a year now I have not experienced a single headache, and my skin remains clear. I've gotten rid of all the old ointments, medicines, allergy shots, and diets. The only thing I've kept are my precious dog-eared papers—those powerful Scripture exercises that brought my faith to life. For there's one thing I've learned: Though it's important to keep physical muscles well-toned, it's even more important to keep "faith muscles" strong. For they are the ones that churn the spiritual energy, that move the mountains in our lives. Even a mountain like mine, which had towered over me for sixteen years.

A few weeks ago at a meeting a stranger tapped my shoulder. "Your complexion is so beautiful," she said.

"Oh, thank you," I said, breaking into an unusually big smile. A smile, I'm sure, no one there really understood . . . except for me and God.

*Tilting the bottle of kerosene unsteadily
with one hand, I opened the lid
with the other.*

GRANNY'S WINGS

COOKIE POTTER, SAN MATEO, CALIFORNIA

When I was five, my great-grandmother lived with us in a big Victorian house in San Francisco. Granny was ninety-two years old, frail, and virtually an invalid; she spent much of her time reading the Bible in her room. Her favorite verse was from Isaiah: "They that wait upon the Lord shall renew their strength; they shall mount up with wings as eagles; they shall run, and not be weary; and they shall walk and not faint" (40:31). Granny couldn't walk unaided.

On those rare occasions when she ventured out of her room, she shuffled slowly, balancing herself by holding on tentatively to the backs of chairs. Granny's bedroom was right next to the kitchen, where Mama usually tended the wood stove and stirred a pot of stew or beans.

One day I was alone in the kitchen, the stove already lit. I had often watched Mama pour in kerosene to start the fire. Flames leaped up in a kaleidoscope of brilliant colors. I thought I'd try pouring some myself.

I pushed a stool close to the stove and climbed up. Tilting the bottle of kerosene unsteadily with one hand, I opened the lid with the other. As I leaned over to pour the fluid, the bottom of my dress brushed the stove top and teased the flames.

Just at that moment Granny shuffled in. One glance told her the danger I was in. She flew across the kitchen and grabbed the kerosene out of my hand, then snatched me off the stool.

That day, she really did fly like an eagle.

MY OWN LIFE IS PROOF

DAN WAKEFIELD, MIAMI BEACH, FLORIDA

I know the truth of Einstein's words; I have lived both ways. Growing up in Indiana in the 1940s, I saw the world with wonder—in the frost on windowpanes, in the winter constellations, in the flowers called four-o'clocks that opened around that hour on summer afternoons. Attending Baptist Bible school, I watched in awe as a young preacher and his wife made miracles come to life, using a brown paper bag over a drinking fountain to reenact the story of when Moses drew water from a rock.

As a young writer living in New York City's Greenwich Village in the 1950s, numbing myself with bourbon and Freud (the former a daily habit and the latter a six-year, five-times-a-week psychoanalysis), I saw the world through a darker lens. With sincere, if self-conscious, cynicism, I adopted an Ernest Hemingway character's prayer of nothingness: Our nada who art in nada. My newfound view of Bible stories was expressed by a pseudo-jaded friend, who had gone to a more enlightened sort of Sunday school, where she was taught scientific explanations of the miracles in the Bible. Just how had Moses led the Israelites across the Red Sea? She explained while exhaling two tusks of cigarette smoke: "Low tide."

Clearly, I was at low tide myself by 1980. Several years earlier I had left both my home in Boston and the woman I had hoped to spend the rest of my life with. I had moved to Hollywood to write an NBC series called *James at 15*. Before that, I had worked as a journalist and author for publications such as *The Atlantic Monthly, Esquire, Harper's Magazine,* and *The Nation*. I had had four novels published; one of them,

Starting Over, was made into a movie starring Candice Bergen and Burt Reynolds.

But in southern California, surrounded by palm trees and people whose satisfaction in life was dependent on Nielsen ratings and box office revenues, I felt things falling apart. When *James at 15* was canceled, I stayed on in California to struggle at the entertainment business, constantly drinking to soothe the stress. That created even greater stress and a resting pulse of 120, a condition called tachycardia. I tried to write, but it became impossible. My attention span was getting shorter and my money was getting lower. My life consisted of the nothingness Hemingway's fictional character discovered. Yet mine was real.

I was a few dreary weeks away from my forty-eighth birthday when I woke up screaming one morning. It was more than a nightmare. Wide awake, I got out of bed and screamed some more. In misery and despair I groped among a pile of old books and pulled out a Bible I hadn't opened since high school, except for research. I turned to the Psalms, that source of comfort and sustenance to people for more than 2000 years, and read aloud the Twenty-third Psalm.

Throughout the weeks ahead I repeated that Psalm again and again. "He leadeth me beside the still waters. . . ." In the spring of 1980 I got on a plane and returned to Boston, where I went like a homing pigeon to sit on a bench beside the still waters of the pond in the Public Garden.

A new journey for me had begun. I joined a church called King's Chapel and began attending an adult Bible study. I started a steady program of exercise and a healthy diet. By 1984 I was able to give up the constant drinking that had been my addiction—indeed my very identity. But even more amazing, I became free of the desire to drink. The need that had once consumed me was gone, lifted. One of the definitions of the word *miracle* is an extraordinary event "considered as a work of God," and that's how I felt—and still do—about my release from alcohol. There was no doubt: I had experienced a miracle.

Step by step I continued on my way. My minister, the Reverend Carl Scovel, pointed out that the translation of conversion in both Hebrew and Greek is "turning." When you turn even slightly you are going a different way, and the further you go the more distant your old way becomes. Instead of a driven, frantic existence, I was gradually changing my perspective, looking inward and focusing on a healthier and more spiritual way.

At the King's Chapel parish house, I sat with nine others around a table as Carl Scovel led us in a class about writing a spiritual autobiography. Difficult as it was in the beginning, I slowly began to share my most intimate fears and struggles— and learned that others too had gone through a dark night of the soul. Eventually I started leading workshops myself.

I now saw that a spiritual path really is a path, a genuine ongoing journey, and not just a metaphor. My new path was taking me to churches and adult-education centers around the country to guide others in writing their own spiritual autobiographies. I helped people of all ages and backgrounds as they poured out their deepest feelings on paper.

My personal satisfaction was enormous. But by 1993 I was out of writing ideas—and cash. All spring I had worked on a novel, and when people I trusted told me it wasn't good, I threw it away. "I'm in trouble," I said to a friend. "I need a miracle."

One day not long after, my phone rang. It was a call from an editor in San Francisco. "We've got a great book idea and we want you to write it," he said. What was the subject? Miracles.

"I've got a head start on this one," I told the editor excitedly. I contacted the people I knew from my workshops and asked them to send me stories of what they considered miracles in their own lives.

Next I set out to interview on my own. A woman in Atlanta told me her daughter had suffered a traumatic brain injury when hit by a car and was given little hope for recovery. Yet with prayer from family, friends, and Bible study groups, the girl came out of her coma and returned to school and a full life.

A friend in Los Angeles who had suffered third-degree burns and was scheduled for skin-graft operations met with psychologists and medical assistants who were experimenting with alternative healing. The morning after the group had moved their hands above her body in "energy techniques," the burns were gone. (The surgeon who was to do the skin grafts insisted there was no way such a healing could have happened. It happened.)

Rabbi Nancy Flam, one of the founders of the Jewish Healing Center in San Francisco, believes that healing can occur through "the ministry of presence," by clearing one's mind to be fully present to another human being. When we give others our full and loving attention, we become "a conduit for Divinity to express itself." Or, as Thérèse of Lisieux put it in the nineteenth century, "Whose hands are God's hands but our hands?"

In Athlone, Ireland, I met a glowing, rosy-cheeked woman named Marion Carroll. Others attested to the fact that she had suffered from multiple sclerosis, was blind in one eye, had lost control of her bodily functions, and had been paralyzed in her legs for three years. In 1989 she was taken on a stretcher to a shrine in Ireland. She heard a whispery voice tell her to get up, and when she did, "My legs weren't even stiff!" She hasn't needed a wheelchair or catheter since. "My healin' does not belong to me," she reported. "It's a special gift to people . . . to let them know . . . God's work is happenin' now—like when he walked among us."

But what about people who are not cured? I discovered an even deeper kind of miracle in their stories. Lloyd Kantor, a Vietnam vet who lost both arms and legs and one eye in the war, married and went to Paris on his honeymoon, then took a trip to Tahiti. He and his wife, Loretta, returned to Mount

Vernon, New York, to do volunteer work. They arranged to have ramps put in the city hall and an elevator in the town library and to have a memorial erected bearing the names of local men who died in Vietnam. "All in all, things have worked out well," Lloyd told me in a firm, strong voice. "I have to believe it has to do with God."

I discovered that many artists consider their creativity miraculous. While on a visit to Germany, writer Marcie Hershman was dramatically struck by "a silence full of voices still calling out" that reminded her of relatives who had died in the Holocaust; it led her to write two searing novels about that time, *Tales of the Master Race* and *Safe in America*. "In the Bible, miracles aren't confined just to blessings of joy," Marcie told me. "Some are about evil and how to confront it rather than turn away." Marcie's ability to deal with such a challenge was, to her, a miracle.

Other artists described to me the state of grace they felt on occasions when they transmitted something higher—or what William Blake described as the feeling that his poems were dictated by the angels.

At the same time, we are surrounded by miracles every day. "We see people looking for weeping statues," said Frankie Murray, a curate in County Longford, Ireland. "They miss the every morning miracles—like the sunrise and friendship."

Or the frost on the windowpane in my long-ago Hoosier boyhood. In a sense my path has taken me full circle, back to the simple wonderment at God's mighty hand in the winter constellations. As Willa Cather has written, "Miracles . . . rest not so much upon faces or voices or healing power coming suddenly near to us from afar off, but upon our perceptions being made finer, so that for a moment our eyes can see and our ears can hear what is there about us always."

As for me, I proceed day by day on my journey as a writer and teacher. There is no doubt that miracles abound. The path my own life has taken is proof.

*I began to wonder if faith and prayer
had a hand in helping us heal.*

THE HEALING EFFECT

DALE A. MATTHEWS, M.D., WASHINGTON, D.C.

After suffering incapacitating migraines for thirty years, Feliciana came to me for treatment. She taught emotionally troubled high-school students in the inner city and had a passion for her work—perhaps too much. "Do you take your problems home with you at night and on weekends?" I asked.

"Yes," she admitted. "I worry about my students all the time, and I'm always anxious that I'm not doing enough for them."

I'd already given Feliciana a prescription for the latest migraine medication. But I took my pad, wrote another note and handed it to her. She looked surprised at what I had prescribed: "Come to me all you that are weary and are carrying heavy burdens, and I will give you rest" (Matthew 11:28).

As an associate professor of medicine at Georgetown University School of Medicine, I have studied and compiled a large body of data about the effect of faith on physical healing. In addition, years of observing my patients' experiences have convinced me of an important clinical finding: The words of the Bible can have a healing effect on my patients' physical and emotional recovery.

I wasn't always so confident about introducing this sort of treatment into my practice. Early in my medical career, I was taken aback by a patient who came to me with an unusual request.

"I want you to pray with me," he said. I blurted out a quick prayer so we could return to what I then considered more solid medical ground.

Despite my doubts, the prayer clearly had a calming effect

on my patient, and I began to wonder if faith and prayer had a hand in helping us heal. Gradually more and more patients— perhaps noticing the Bible I now kept on my shelf alongside my medical journals—requested that I pray with them. I started to look to the Bible as well as my Physician's Desk Reference and prescription pad as tools of my trade.

When the Bible says "Direct me in the path of your commands, for there I find delight" (Psalm 119:35), it seems to be literally true—and delight certainly offers a positive state receptive to healing. Steady doses of "Be strong, and of good courage. Fear not . . . " (I Chronicles 22:13) can be beneficial for someone facing surgery.

"Let not your heart be troubled . . . " (John 14:1) may do wonders for someone worrying about the toll of a chronic incapacitation or developing illness. After all, "Pleasant words are as a honeycomb, sweet to the soul, and health to the bones" (Proverbs 16:24).

Another reason the Bible helps people get better is because it enables them to reframe their problems in a more constructive way.

I noticed this in the case of Barbara (I've changed all my patients' names for this story), a thirty-one-year-old with cancer, who related to the story of the woman in the Book of Matthew who was healed by Jesus when she touched the hem of his robe. One day while taking communion Barbara visualized an encounter of her own with Christ and was flooded with a deep sense of peace that overcame the anxiety that had been plaguing her during her therapy.

Another of my patients, Ron, suffered from an extreme depression that was holding back his physical healing from the ravages of alcoholism. I said, "Think about some stories of Bible heroes who got depressed, such as Saul, David and the Apostle Paul." I reminded him that even "Jesus wept." Once Ron reframed his experience and understood it was a difficulty he shared with others, even great figures of faith, he was able to let go of his feelings of shame and proceed with treatment.

Louisa, battling persistent fatigue, learned from the story of the prophet Elijah that God could speak to her in "a still small voice" (I Kings 19:12). In order to hear God fully, she realized she needed to make time in her hectic routine for quiet contemplation. She rearranged her priorities in a way that affected her whole life and bolstered her recovery.

Another patient, Claire, was critically ill with endocarditis, a bacterial infection of the heart lining, when I first met her in the emergency room. "You don't have to be religious to use the Bible for medicine," I explained. "Find a verse, a bit of Scripture that appeals to you, and repeat it on your daily walks." Of course timely medical intervention played a part in her impressive recovery. But Claire has no doubt repeating Bible verses helped too, and her spiritual life continues to develop.

What guidelines go along with my "prescriptions"?

Dosage. A daily dose of Bible reading is what I recommend. Like most medications, it's helpful to get in the habit of taking it at the same time every day. When I do it as part of my morning routine, my day is always off to a good start.

How long to take? There's no cutoff point. I advise patients to develop healthy patterns for the rest of their lives—exercise, eat a balanced diet, get enough rest. And continue to read the Bible—indefinitely. It's long-term therapy.

What's the cost? No escalating prices here. You don't need

a referral from health-insurance agencies, and in the Bible's case, the primary-care physician is always in.

Preventive medicine. There are common-sense warnings against excessive intake of fats, alcohol, or any food or activity that we indulge in to the point our lives are thrown out of physical and mental balance. Whether about warding off depression ("The cheerful heart has a continual feast" Proverbs 15:15) or getting the necessary rest ("Remember the Sabbath . . . you shall not do any work . . ." Exodus 20:8, 10), the Bible is full of sound advice.

What happened to my teacher friend Feliciana's migraines? I pointed out to her that it's fine to be conscientious, but, ultimately, "taking care of those students is God's job, not yours. As you leave school each afternoon, say a prayer turning the students over to God's care. If you worry about them in the evening, remind yourself they are in God's hands. And He is giving you the strength and wisdom to guide them."

On her next visit Feliciana reported that my prescriptions were working. Today, in much-improved health, Feliciana is teaching with new vitality.

As a physician, I believe we can effectively aid our healing by turning to God with a willing heart. That's why among the latest medical books lining my office, there will always be a place for the Holy Bible, the great handbook of healing.

95

TRUSTING
GOD

Miracles only work through your own faith.

PAPA RAMDAS

NOT ON THE MENU

IMOGENE WAGSTER, COLUMBIA, TENNESSEE

One day after eating shrimp salad, I itched everywhere, my lips swelled, and my throat began to close. "You're allergic to the iodine in shrimp," my family doctor said. "Don't eat it again."

Several years later I was admitted to the hospital for surgery. God, I'm so nervous. Please be with me. Among the forms I was given to complete was the menu for dinner, and shrimp was one of the choices. Of course I crossed it off and chose another entrée. Later the anesthesiologist asked if I was allergic to any medications. "I'm allergic to shrimp," I said. Ordinarily I wouldn't have thought to mention foods, but because of the menu, it was on my mind. The anesthesiologist scrawled something on my chart and left.

That afternoon I was wheeled off and given a purple dye to drink for a test. But a nurse suddenly appeared and stopped me. "Your test has been canceled," she said.

My surgery proceeded and I awoke to hear that everything went well. "But it's a good thing you told us about your shrimp allergy and we canceled that test," my doctor said. "There's iodine in the purple dye and the consequences could have been disastrous."

When the dietitian came to discuss my meals that evening I told her how thankful I was that shrimp had been on the hospital menu the day before.

She looked at me strangely. "That couldn't have been," she said. "We never serve shrimp to our patients."

*Needles, syringes, and tubes
all blurred together. I felt as if
my chest were being crushed.*

HEALING TOUCH

AMANDA PERRY, VALDOSTA, GEORGIA

I was thirteen years old when I figured out what I wanted to be when I grew up. My bulldog, Bonnie, was pregnant, and we went to our veterinarian so he could deliver her puppies. I stood close by, watching as the vet performed a cesarean section and pulled the first puppy from Bonnie's belly. He placed it in my hands. "Rub his back until he starts to breathe," he told me. I massaged the puppy carefully. Suddenly a spasm shook his body and his wrinkly little face turned pink. He squealed softly as if to say hello. I was hooked. What could be better than holding one of God's creatures in your hands and helping it take its first breath?

I suppose it wasn't too surprising I wanted to work with animals. I had grown up on our family farm in southern Georgia, helping herd the cattle, saving scraps of food for my pet guinea pigs, running with my dog along the rows of cotton. After high school, I enrolled in the pre-vet program at the University of Georgia. A crop failure at home made money tight, but Mama was determined that wouldn't get in the way of my goal. She prayed about it with her prayer group and got the idea to start breeding bulldogs and Persian cats to help pay for my schooling.

I went on to vet school, working odd jobs in the summers to keep ahead of tuition costs. During vet school Mama gave me one of her bulldogs, Pokey. Each day, when I came home from class and she nuzzled her face into my hands, I was reminded of how much I loved animals, how I couldn't wait to help pets whose owners treasured them as much as I did my Pokey.

In junior year, it was time to start surgery lab. I pulled on those tight, thin latex gloves doctors use and set to work. After the first class, I noticed my hands looked kind of splotchy. I figured it was because they were sweating from nervousness.

But each day after lab my hands looked worse. First they became swollen, then they started to crack and bleed. I showed them to my instructor. "Probably just dry skin," he said. "Try putting some udder balm on them." I did, but my hands got no better. On a visit to Mama and Daddy, Mama saw my hands and said, "They must feel awful, Amanda."

"It's okay, Mama," I said. "Just as long as I can do all the lab procedures."

But then in late 1996, when I was in my last year of vet school, I had to have minor surgery. During the operation I broke out in hives. Later my doctor inquired about my red and blistered palms, and eventually he put two and two together. "You have a latex allergy," he told me. "I'll give you some medicine to treat the symptoms, but each time that you are exposed to latex, the reaction gets more powerful. You ought to stay away from it altogether."

So when I graduated in May and took a job at a veterinary clinic in Valdosta, I explained my allergy to my employer, and he agreed to let me special order a brand of more expensive, non-latex gloves.

"Are your hands still bothering you, honey?" Mama asked one day not long after I started at the clinic. She took my hands in hers and examined them gently.

"Just a bit," I answered. "They're better than before."

I figured a little discomfort was a small price to pay for being able to do what I'd always wanted. I loved the parade of cats and dogs I greeted each day: cocker spaniels and Chihuahuas, tabbies and Siamese. Best of all was delivering a healthy litter of puppies or kittens.

I had to go into the hospital again for another surgery. I made sure I informed the doctor of my allergy, but by accident I was given an injection from a syringe that had been inserted through a latex stopper. Suddenly my throat started closing up. The staff rushed to get my breathing under control.

I'd never had a reaction like that before, and it scared me. I went back to work, but I noticed myself having more reactions.

When I was working on a dog or cat, my hands and face would break out in a rash and I started coughing. Again I'd get that scary feeling of my throat swelling shut.

"What's happening to me?" I asked Mama one evening. "It seems like everything I touch these days makes me sick."

"We just have to keep trusting in your doctors and in the Lord," she said.

My doctors sent me to see a specialist to help pin down what was causing my reactions. I had a full set of allergy tests done. The allergist looked over my chart for a few moments, then said, "Dr. Perry, as you know you're strongly allergic to latex. But you're also allergic to many grasses and pollens. Most importantly, you're allergic to dogs and cats."

I almost laughed out loud. "No, that can't be," I said, shaking my head. "I've been around dogs and cats all my life."

"Yes, but your latex allergy has affected your whole immune system so that you've become allergic to other things too." He paused. "As allergic as you are to dogs and cats, I don't think you'll be able to practice veterinary medicine for much longer."

I felt that same surge of panic as when my throat closed up

during those reactions. "But I've dreamed about being a veterinarian since I was a child," I said. "I can't quit."

"I'm afraid you'll have to."

I could barely contain myself until I left the office. As soon as I saw Mama waiting for me in the parking lot, I burst into tears. I told her what the doctor had said. "I can't quit now, not after how hard we've both worked," I said. "I just can't."

Mama held me silently for a long time until I'd calmed down, then said, "This is just one of those things we're going to turn over to the Lord, Amanda."

God, I prayed frantically, please don't let me have to give up my dream. Help me beat this somehow.

My doctors increased my allergy-medication doses, but even so, when I operated on a dog or cat, I'd get congested and weak. Often my throat would start to close up and I'd have to stop and give myself a shot of epinephrine to counteract the allergic reaction.

At my doctor's insistence, I finally took Pokey to live with my parents, thinking that if at least my home were free of allergens, I could manage the ones at work. "I'll miss you, baby," I whispered to her before hurrying out to my car, trying not to look at her big sad eyes in the rearview mirror as I headed back to my empty house.

Still my reactions persisted, as bad as ever. By the summer of 1999, I was taking twenty different pills to control my allergies. Every couple of weeks, I still ended up in the hospital, where they'd set up a latex-free isolation room for me. I could not even drive anymore because of the danger of passing out from a reaction while on the road. Mama drove me everywhere and stayed with me through every hospital visit.

Why is this happening to me, God? I couldn't help but keep asking. Why don't you make me well again?

Reluctantly I agreed to my doctor's advice and went on job disability for six months. I started a program of allergy shots to desensitize myself to animals. Then I took the hardest step of all. I called a local college and set up an appointment for the next month to take aptitude tests so that I might try and find a new career.

"The only jobs I want involve animals," I said to Mama one afternoon. "I can't even work with farm animals because of all my environmental allergies. There's nothing left for me to do."

"I wish I could help you somehow, Amanda," said Mama. "All I know to do is to keep praying."

"I keep asking God to make me better so I can go back to doing what He prepared me to do. But nothing changes."

"Sometimes I ask Him to help you keep being a vet too. Sometimes I ask Him to convince you to quit. It's hard to know sometimes the best thing to do," Mama said. "Maybe you should ask God what He wants you to do now, which path He wants you to take."

I saw only one path. I had to keep trying every treatment I possibly could until I got back to normal again. Being a veterinarian was a huge part of who I was. I couldn't think about a future without that.

On November 11, 1999, after Mama drove me to an appointment with a specialist, I felt a bad reaction beginning.

"Mama, get me to the hospital," I said. "Quick."

I was rushed into an isolation room at the hospital. My hands were so swollen I couldn't bend my fingers around Mama's hand. Needles, syringes, and tubes all blurred together.

I felt as if my chest were being crushed. Then I heard, "Amanda, this is Dr. Jarrell. We're going to put a tube down your throat to help you breathe."

And then instantly I was in a wonderful white place, like a room of clouds, and I saw a brilliant, soothing presence moving toward me. I knew immediately it was Jesus. The light enveloped me and I felt a calm I'd never experienced before.

The next thing I knew I was in a hospital bed again. When I opened my eyes I saw my mother's face. I tried to talk but the tube was still down my throat.

Mama leaned over me and asked if I knew that I had died. I nodded. She said that the doctors had given me ten jolts of the defibrillator paddles to get my heart beating again. "They worked on you for fifteen minutes. We thought you were gone. Dr. Adcock said there was nothing more he could do, but then we all gathered around your bed and prayed. When you came back to us, we knew our prayers had been answered." Still, Mama said the doctors were concerned about my condition.

"Everyone's praying for you," Mama said. "You just rest."

Don't worry, Mama, I'm going to be all right, I wanted to

tell her. I knew with complete certainty that God held me safely in His hands.

The doctors were amazed to find I had suffered no permanent brain damage. I was released from the hospital just a few days later and spent several weeks recuperating at home, away from anything that could cause me allergic reactions. I missed animals, but I realized now that I could go on without them, if that was necessary. God would take care of my future just as surely as He had taken care of my life.

Mama and I were flown to the Mayo Clinic in Minnesota by a volunteer service called Angel Flight of Georgia so I could be treated by one of the few latex-allergy specialists in the country.

Slowly, the doctor weaned me off the strong medicines I was taking, one by one. Then he gave me a full checkup. "Amanda," he said, "you're not going to believe this, but the allergy tests all came back negative."

Just like when I was first told about all my allergies, I broke into tears. So did Mama. We went home, and I slowly began to spend time around animals. One hot summer day I was well enough to drive to my parents' house to visit Pokey. She came bounding up to my truck. I reached out to pick her up and her whole body seemed to wag with joy.

Last October I returned to the veterinary clinic after an eleven-month leave of absence. Everything looked so new and clean—the stainless-steel exam table, the cotton swabs, the syringes, the bottles of neatly labeled medicine. I felt like I was starting over.

I still stay away from latex, but I'm back at work full-time now. And I'm no longer afraid to take a different path if I feel that's what God wants. Often when I hold a newborn puppy or kitten in my hands, I think back to being cradled in that white light, the moment when God revealed to me that my life—and my future—have always been safe in His hands.

A HAILSTORM OF HEALING

SALLY H. ROBBINS, BRISTOL, TENNESSEE

What I remember most about the summer of 1934, when Dad got his tonsils out, is how hot it was. The middle of July in Blackwood, Virginia, and we hadn't seen a drop of rain or felt a cool breeze for days. The ground was parched, the flowers drooping. Normally, I could at least cool down with an ice-cold drink. The ice man hadn't been around, though, and the last block of ice in our icebox had long since melted.

Dad was recovering from his operation in the downstairs bedroom when Mom rushed out to the kitchen telephone. She called the doctor's office. "He's hemorrhaging badly," she said, urgency in her voice. "What can we do?" Then I heard her repeat the doctor's instructions. "Ice. Make a compress of ice and pack it around his throat."

But there was no ice for miles around. We lived ten miles from town. Dad couldn't be moved and Mom didn't dare leave him. She tried wrapping Dad's neck with cloths drenched in cold water, but it was no use. His throat kept swelling and he was still bleeding. Tears filling her eyes, Mom said brokenly, "Lord, you take over. I'm lost." I was worried so I wailed a prayer of my own. "God, please help my daddy. Please!"

Mom took me in her arms just as the wind began to blow. The sky grew dark as dusk, then simply opened up. The hammering noise on the roof was deafening. Mom kissed me on the forehead. She grabbed a pail and ran outside. Soon she was back, and in fifteen minutes Dad's bleeding had been stopped by the large balls of ice she'd collected from the heaven-sent hailstorm.

*At seventy-seven, I was facing
major surgery—open-heart surgery.*

A CHANGED MAN

ART CARNEY, WESTBROOK, CONNECTICUT

O ne morning two years ago I was taking out the trash when I felt a quick, sharp pain in my chest. What was that? I wondered, a bit scared for the obvious reason. I tried to shrug it off as just a passing ache of old age. Maybe a muscle spasm or heartburn. Nothing to worry about, I assured myself. And surely nothing to worry anyone else about. Back inside the house, the pain faded.

I'm not one to confide my troubles, even to my wife, Jean, though if I do turn to someone it's she. Most people assume actors are garrulous and outgoing, but without a script in my hand I'm often at a loss for words. Besides, I didn't want to scare Jean or make a fuss out of something that was probably no big deal. Best not to dwell on it.

Then one pleasant day I drove to Bradley International Airport to meet a friend who had come to visit. I had grabbed her two large bags from the luggage belt and was walking to our car when I suddenly felt as if a fist were clenching my heart. I put the bags down for a second to catch my breath. Jean and our friend were up ahead, busily chatting. Again I decided to stay silent. The pain would pass, I was sure, and by the time I threw the bags in the trunk of our car it had. But the memory lingered; and a week later, when the tightness in my chest returned, sharper and longer this time and with no precipitating physical strain, I finally confessed to Jean, "I think we'd better see a doctor."

We went to Dr. Stephen Franklin, a well-recommended cardiologist. Laid-back and reassuring, Dr. Franklin couldn't help but frown when I mentioned that this had not been my first episode of chest pain. "You didn't tell anyone?" he asked, raising an eyebrow and scribbling on my chart.

Over the next couple of weeks I was put on a treadmill for a stress test, underwent an echocardiography and began taking heart medication. Dr. Franklin still wasn't satisfied, and I was getting nervous. One day he asked, "Ever have any leg problems, Art?"

"Some," I answered, tapping my right leg and explaining I had had a total knee implant to alleviate arthritis that had resulted from my catching some German shrapnel on a battlefield in France shortly after D-Day.

"Then we'll have to use your left for the angiogram," he said evenly.

I felt a wave of apprehension break over me, but I just nodded my head and said that was fine.

The procedure started with me swallowing some stuff that smelled like insecticide, followed by the insertion of a catheter-like probe into a leg artery. Dr. Franklin threaded the device up into the chambers of my heart, where he was able to look for arterial blockage. He concentrated intensely on his work. When he was through he gently but firmly informed me that coronary bypass surgery was imperative.

"Don't worry, Art. Bypass surgery has become virtually routine in this day and age. You'll do just fine."

What wasn't routine was that I would require a quintuple bypass.

When I got home that day I retreated to the bedroom, where I could be alone. I started pacing and worrying. At seventy-seven, I was facing major surgery—open-heart surgery. I threw myself into a big easy chair, hoping to harness my racing panic. I stared at the blue walls filled with family photos of Jean, our three children and six grandchildren, sharply aware of how much I loved them.

I could not face this alone. I knew that. I would need my family and I would need the One who was the greatest physician of all. I implored God with all the strength I had, "I have not been one of Your best servants, but I never stopped believing in You. I know Jean is praying. I need You too. Forgive me and help me."

A few days later I was admitted to Hartford Hospital. My

anxiety diminished considerably when I met Dr. Hiroyoshi Takata, the man who would operate on me. He was open and unassuming; I sensed at once God had placed me in good hands.

While I waited on a gurney in pre-op the morning of my surgery, Jean and our children, Eileen, Brian and Paul, prayed. Silently I joined them: "God, please give comfort to my family." Then I was wheeled into the operating room.

The surgery went well and by the next day I was put into step-down intensive care, for patients who are expected to recover without complications. It was as I lay there in my hospital bed, weak, in pain and uncertain about the future, that I became aware of a figure in the room with me. I was fully conscious, and though I was surprised by his appearance, I was unafraid. The figure stood quietly before me. He was wrapped in a soft, diaphanous material that appeared to be as much air as fabric. I couldn't take my eyes off the figure. My gaze was held by an irresistible attraction. I heard a voice, rich and reassuring, say the words: "You are being given a new beginning."

I leaned closer to the vision and saw . . . me. What I was looking at was a version of myself, healthy, strong, well again. I had a glow to my face. Yes, it was me, a new me. I was filled with peace and joy and a feeling of wellness, wholeness. I realized I had been powerfully blessed by God, shown the gift of health He wanted me to have.

As soon as Jean arrived that day I couldn't stop myself from telling her what had happened. "I was wide awake. I'm certain of it," I said. "This was no dream or hallucination. This was real." She squeezed my hand reassuringly and pressed her cheek to mine.

The strangest thing happened the next morning. I awoke sobbing. I wasn't in pain; I wasn't unhappy. In fact, I felt better than I ever had. I just couldn't stop. I couldn't stop crying a purifying torrent of tears. It felt good, a cosmic sense of relief and release, as if my soul had been bathed in love. Later, Jean said it sounded like "a cleansing of the spirit." I had never heard that expression but I understood it intuitively at once. "Sometimes," she explained, "people who have undergone a religious experience can't stop their tears. It is a kind of blessing."

A religious experience? Is that what I had had? Something had happened, something powerful and irreversible. If it was

God, touching my life with an incredible vision, then I could only believe I was no longer the same person I had been before. I was the person I had been shown.

I recovered with unprecedented swiftness, spending only seven days in the hospital. I went through some tough physical therapy, and today I possess more vigor than I have had in years. The most enduring transformation, however, has been in the way I live. An introvert since childhood, I was most comfortable on stage or on camera. Since that amazing day in the hospital I've been able to open up to the people I love and who love me. I've stopped trying to hide who I am. I don't turn my eyes away from strangers or retreat into silence. And that, more than anything, is a freedom I had never known before.

A healing voice assured me I should have no fear, that I would be well again. I am better than well. I am changed.

WHILE MY PARENTS SLEPT

EMMA WILFORD, SHERMAN OAKS, CALIFORNIA

Religious faith may seem elusive to some people in our modern age, but for me it's never been a problem. It's not just because I was raised by devout Italian immigrants. More important was something I witnessed as a seven-year-old girl living in Cleveland. Ever since that June afternoon more than seventy-five years ago, faith in God's power has been as natural to me as breathing.

I was the fifth of six children born to Paulo Florio and Assunta Ciccarelli, who lived in a wooden frame house on West Sixtieth Street in a sprawling, ethnically mixed neighborhood. Their first child, Dominick, was born in 1904, soon followed by Mary, Rose, Theresa, me, and little Anthony. Papa worked long hours with the Cleveland Railway Co. to support us and wasn't home much. Momma was busy doing laundry, mending clothes, shopping, and cooking—yet I never heard her once complain. She had strong religious faith and took us all to church every Sunday.

My brothers, sisters, and I all looked up to Dom, our big brother. Tall and handsome, Dom had straight black hair parted stylishly down the middle. With large, expressive brown eyes and a beguiling smile, he charmed everyone he met. Never drawn to book-learning, Dom quit school after the eighth grade to make money to help us all out. He worked as a shoe salesman and bought us treats with his weekly salary. Robust and confident, he had never been sick a day in his life. Momma and Papa doted on him, as we all did.

Then, one morning late in the spring of 1920, when Dom

was seventeen, he didn't appear for breakfast. "Where's Dominick?" Momma asked, dishing out our oatmeal.

I put down my spoon and dashed upstairs, peeking around his door. He lay in bed.

"Dom?" I said. He waved at me feebly. "I'm too tired to get up," he said.

Momma appeared and put her hand on his forehead. "He has a fever," she said. She brought cold cloths for his head.

But hour by hour the fever got higher. After two days he became delirious. Thank goodness Papa was home, and he and Momma managed to get Dom to nearby St. John Hospital.

The diagnosis was grim: "Brain fever"—spinal meningitis. Even nowadays this dreaded disease, which mainly strikes children and teenagers, can be fatal or cause permanent brain damage. Back in the 1920s, before antibiotics and other wonder drugs, meningitis had no treatment or cure. When Dom slipped into a coma shortly after being admitted, there was nothing his doctors could do for his condition but advise my parents to pray.

Momma and Papa certainly didn't need any encouragement to do that. Every morning they left for the hospital in hopeful anticipation, but their faces were always strained when they returned home in the late afternoon.

I was only seven, but I knew Dom was very sick. "We sit beside him talking," I heard Momma telling one of my sisters. "For hours. But he can't open his eyes. Or make a sound. Or even move a finger." Papa put his arms around her as she leaned against his chest, softly weeping.

Like our parents, we children prayed hard for Dom to recover. My prayers were sincere, but I have to admit that with each passing day my faith began to weaken. God, why aren't you making Dom well? This has been going on for so long.

Then, on the seventeenth day of his coma, Dom's face began to turn blue. His lungs were failing; his heartbeat was weaker. Dom was dying.

Momma and Papa sat with him for hours, holding his hands and praying. Then they returned home, exhausted from the emotional and physical stress.

I had just gotten back from school when I saw Momma and Papa come in. They were so sad and tired they barely spoke. Momma went right to the bedroom and lay down; when I looked in a minute later, she was fast asleep. While resting on the couch in the living room, Papa had fallen sound asleep too. As I played idly with a doll on the kitchen floor, I looked at the dust motes drifting in the late afternoon sunlight. Why wasn't God making Dom better? Weren't all those prayers from all those people helping? I uttered another one of my own, from deep within my being: "God, please, make my brother well."

I sat in silence for a few minutes, a shiver building along the back of my neck. From far away I heard a dog bark, a window open, a neighbor call out. Then suddenly the stillness was broken. Papa woke with a start. He gave a cry like I had never heard before—"Assunta! Assunta!"—and leaped to his feet. He raced toward the bedroom. At the same time Momma had woken abruptly and leaped out of bed. As I sat on the floor in wonderment, my parents rushed at each other from opposite ends of the house and met in the hallway right in front of me.

"Paulo!" Momma cried. "I just had a dream! I had been praying before I fell asleep and I know the message was from God. A voice told me, 'Go to the hospital! Now!'"

I will never forget the shock in my father's voice. "Assunta, just moments ago I had the same dream. I also heard those words: 'Go to the hospital! Now!'" He threw his arms around my mother. "Hurry!" he said.

My parents rushed to the hospital and went straight to my big brother's room. Dom was sitting upright. He had just come out of the coma. With a weak but clear voice, he said with a smile, "I want some ice cream."

He had recovered. The doctors were astounded. They discharged Dom soon afterward. He went on to live a full, healthy life of eighty years.

Dom later told me that while lying in the coma he had experienced a vision that forever took away his fear of death. But he didn't tell anyone exactly what it was he saw. He only said, "I will never be afraid to die. God is good and I will trust in Him forever."

Many events have occurred in my life since, some involving illness and great disappointment and loss. But my parents' miraculous dreams on that June afternoon gave me the knowledge that God directs our lives in ways we cannot begin to fathom. And, like Dominick, I will trust in Him forever.

It was as if the house were killing her.
Eventually, we realized there
was only one solution.

126

A SAFE PLACE

CHRISTOPHER DAVIS, NEW YORK, NEW YORK

Imagine what it would be like if the gas in your stove made you sick, if the aftershave your husband wore gave you migraines, if you were afraid to clean the kitchen counter or to do the laundry. That's what life is like for Michele Owen. She has a mysterious condition, multiple chemical sensitivity, also called environmental illness, which affects her immune system and makes her extremely allergic to many ordinary household substances others would use without a thought.

Michele has always suffered from bad allergies. Growing up, she learned to skip foods like milk and fruit, and avoid animal dander. But three years ago, when she moved into a house in an Atlanta subdivision with her husband, Bill, and their baby boy, Avery, she suddenly took a turn for the worse. She could not sleep at all, night or day. She lost almost twenty pounds. Every joint in her body became so sore her slightest movement was slow and painful.

"It felt like the house was attacking me," Michele says.

The gas heat, the stove, the carpet-cleaning chemicals, the closets full of dry-cleaned clothes —all of them posed a health threat for Michele. So she and her husband shut off the gas and cooked on a portable electric stove. Then they got rid of their mattress and bought an organic one that had no flame retardants. They started parking their car out on the street so that the exhaust fumes wouldn't seep into the house from the attached garage.

"But Michele's health was still deteriorating," Bill says. "It was as if the house were killing her. Eventually, we realized there was only one solution. We needed to build a new house, one specially designed for her condition. But how? We didn't know where to begin and we did not have much money. All we could do was rely on God for help and try our best to find a solution."

A friend gave them the busines card of a local builder, John Maxwell, with a quote from Matthew on it: "Take my yoke upon you and learn from me, for I am gentle and humble in heart and you will find rest for your souls." Why did this carpenter have a Bible quote on his card? They sat down with John and explained their problem.

"John got really excited," Michele says. "When he described the kind of house he wanted to build us and how he'd do it, I felt as if, for the first time in a long time, I had a real option. If we built this house I could live a healthy life."

"John made it clear it would be expensive, though," Bill adds. "All the floors had to be hardwood, and the cabinets and doors had to be made of wood, without any glue products or foam inserts. The paint had to be a pricey non-toxic kind. We needed an intensive air-filtration system that uses ultraviolet light to kill germs. I didn't see how we could do it all on our budget. But John told us to decide what kind of house we wanted and find some land. He would get it built."

The Owens found an undeveloped plot for sale in their own subdivision. It was valued at $40,000, but the company that owned the land needed to get rid of it, and they offered to let the Owens have it for $20,000.

"It was right in our price range," Bill says. "We felt like that was a sign there was someone looking after us."

"I started shopping around for building materials," John says. "When I told my subcontractors and suppliers about Michele's condition, many offered to help." The grading company dropped the price of excavating and leveling. Plumbers did the same for their services. One company donated a fireplace, and another some fencing. And the folks at the local bank waived their fees for the construction loan. "All in their own ways were helping me care for my sick wife," Bill says.

The foundation was laid in January, and the work went quickly after that. John Maxwell was able to bring in the project for thousands less than he'd imagined possible. He even had enough left over to build a freestanding garage with an office for

Bill. The Owens moved in at the end of April.

"I've had no allergic reactions to the house at all," Michele says. "It may be years before my body recovers, but I feel so much better now knowing I have a safe place to live. I still can't imagine how we did it, but for the first time in years, I've been able to find rest for my body and for my soul." Thanks to her husband and their builder, her home is a true sanctuary, just as the business card suggested it would be.

3

JOURNEY ON GOOD FRIDAY

FREDA CREAGER, COLORADO SPRINGS, COLORADO

F reda, this looks like a good day to plant those seeds," my husband, John, said as he left for his barbershop.

That afternoon, in the sunshine's warmth, I knelt in the garden planting sweet-pea seeds. It was Good Friday, and the hour when most people in town were at church.

I was still recovering from a serious operation. The doctor didn't think I would walk again. I could only get around with the aid of a walker, and I felt slow, awkward, frustrated. My recovery seemed far away.

"Why Good Friday?" I wondered. For Jesus it had been a day of sadness, pain.

Crawling slowly on my knees, I poked a finger into the earth, dropped in a seed, then covered it.

"Soon shoots will be popping through the spring snow," I told myself. I pictured them, could almost smell their fragrance.

In my garden I felt very near to God. I thought of Christ praying in the Garden of Gethsemane. And as I struggled on my knees, my thoughts traveled with Jesus to his trial, then to Golgotha, where He suffered on the cross. I remembered his cry, "It is finished."

I too had suffered, had lingered near death after brain surgery. Only my faith and my family had sustained me.

Working in the soil, I felt at peace and strengthened. Tucking in the last seed, I stood and gazed proudly at my neat row. "Well, it's finished."

My thoughts remained on Good Friday as I walked to the house. At the porch, I glanced back at my garden.

Then I saw, standing among the rows . . . "My walker!" I gasped. I had walked without it. And I haven't needed it since.

MIRACLES
FROM PRAYER

Amazing things start happening when we start praying!

AUTHOR UNKNOWN

A FULL RECOVERY

KAREN WHITLEY, PORT ANGELES, WASHINGTON

Although I had endured intense pain in my leg for months, I had put off going to the doctor. I was terrified he'd tell me I needed an operation. "I can't believe you waited so long," he chided me when I finally went. "Your leg is bothering you because a disk in your back is pressing on a nerve ending. We'll schedule surgery for next week." Even after he explained every detail of the procedure to my husband, Dave, and me, I was still a nervous wreck. I prayed for comfort all the way into the operating room, until the anesthesia took effect.

When I came to in the recovery room afterward, I didn't know where I was or why a nurse hovered over me. My vision was so foggy I could barely make out "Alice" on the nurse's name tag, and her face was a blur. But her voice comforted me.

"Did everything go okay?" I asked weakly.

Alice took my hand, saying, "Your operation was successful. The ruptured disk has been removed. I spoke to your husband, and he'll be up in a minute." She smiled as she stroked my hand and I drifted off to sleep, soothed and relieved.

When I awoke, Dave was sitting on the edge of my hospital bed. I was so glad to see him! After I repeated everything Alice had told me, I noticed his puzzled expression. Suddenly it dawned on me that I had understood everything she'd said, down to the last detail. You see, I'm deaf and, although I lip-read, with my vision blurred there was no way I could have made out anything my nurse uttered. And yet I'd heard every word!

Sometime during the night,
Frank's kidneys had failed. Janice and
I rushed to the hospital again.

I SAW THE HAND OF GOD MOVE

JOE STEVENSON, RENO, NEVADA

I have always believed in God. But over the years my beliefs about who God is—and what He can do—have changed. It wasn't until my son was gravely ill that I learned you can believe in God and yet not know Him at all.

Know. Knowledge. Logic. When I was younger, those were the words I wanted to live by. As a child I contracted scarlet fever, and this illness ruled out my ever playing sports or roughhousing around. The only real adventures I could go on were adventures of the mind. I read books with a vengeance—great books of the Western World, the volumes of Will and Ariel Durant, and literally thousands more—and out of my reading I formed my strongest beliefs. I believed in logic, in the mind's ability to put all creation into neat, rational categories.

At the same time I was growing up in a strongly Christian family, and so I believed in God. But I insisted—and my insistence caused a lot of arguments—that God Himself was also a being bound by logic and His own natural laws. I guess I pictured God as a great scientist. Miracles? No, God couldn't and wouldn't break laws in that way. When my family told me that Christianity means faith in a loving, miracle-working God, I turned away and went looking for other religions—ones that respected the rational mind above all.

As I became a man, my belief in rationality helped me in my career. I became a salesman for the Bell System, and when I needed to formulate sales strategies and targets, logic unlocked a lot of doors on the way to success.

But other doors seemed to be closed. I felt dry, spiritually empty, and anxious. I tried meditation, ESP, and so on, but the emptiness increased to despair.

In utter defeat, I turned to God in prayer. His Spirit answered with, "I don't simply want belief that I exist. I want you, your will, your life, your dreams, your goals, your very being. And I want your faith, faith that I am sufficient for all your needs." My despair overcame my logic and I yielded all to Him. But just saying you have faith is not the same as having it. In my mind, I still had God in a box.

Maybe that's why I never thought to pray when my oldest son, Frank, came home from first grade one day and said he did not feel well. What would God care about stomach flu?

A doctor with whom my wife Janice and I had consulted wasn't very alarmed about Frank's illness at first. "It's really not too serious," the doctor assured us, "just a bad case of the flu complicated by a little acidosis. Give him this medicine and in a few days he'll be fine."

But Frank wasn't fine, not at all. The medicine worked for a day or so, but then his symptoms—the gagging, choking, and vomiting—came back more violently. His small, six-year-old frame was bathed in sweat and racked with convulsions. We checked him into the local hospital for further testing, but later in the evening our doctor said the original diagnosis was correct. "He's just got a real bad case of it," we were told.

I went to work the next day fully expecting to take Frank and Janice home that night, but when I stopped at the hospital to pick them up, our doctor was there to meet me. "I'd like to have a word with you two," he said, showing Janice and me into a private room.

4

"A problem, Doctor?" I asked.

"Further testing has shown our previous diagnosis was incorrect. We think your son has acute nephritis. It's a terminal kidney disease . . ." He paused, and I could feel the blood running from my face. "But we've found that in children there's a good chance of recovery. Your son has a 90 percent chance of being as good as new."

But by ten o'clock the next morning the news was worse. Sometime during the night, Frank's kidneys had failed. Janice and I rushed to the hospital again.

"X-rays show Frank's kidneys are so badly infected that no

fluid will pass through them," we were told. "The odds aren't in his favor anymore. If those kidneys don't start working within forty-eight hours, I'm afraid your son will die."

I looked at Janice, watching the tears well in her eyes as a huge lump formed in my throat. I took her hand in mine and slowly we walked back to Frank's room. We were too shocked, too upset to even talk. All afternoon we sat at Frank's bedside, watching, stroking his matted blond hair, wiping his damp forehead. The stillness of the room was broken only by the beeps and blips of the machines monitoring little Frank's condition. Specialists would occasionally come, adjust a few tubes, make some marks on Frank's chart, and then silently go. I searched their eyes for an answer, for some glimmer of hope, and got nothing. When our minister came to pray for our son, I could only cry in desperation.

Late that evening, after Frank was asleep, we went home. Friends were waiting with a hot meal, words of encouragement, and news of a vast prayer chain they had begun. And for a fleeting moment, I thought I saw in Janice's eyes the spark of hope that I had been looking for from the doctors all afternoon.

By the following morning, that spark of hope had ignited a flame of confidence in Janice. "I turned Frank's life over to God last night," she told me excitedly, before we were even out of bed. "I feel a real peace about what's going to happen, that God's will is going to be done."

"God's will?" I said angrily. "What kind of God makes little boys get sick? He doesn't care!" And I rolled over. Peace? God's will? No, little Frank would need more than that to get well.

But my anger didn't stop me from trying to reason with God. All that morning, while Janice kept a hospital vigil, I begged and pleaded and screamed at God, daring Him to disprove my skepticism, trying to goad Him into action.

"Who do You think You are?" I shouted once. "Why are You doing this to my son? He's only six! Everybody says You're such a loving God—why don't You show it?" I yelled until I was exhausted. Finally, convinced my arguments were falling on deaf ears, I took our other children to a neighbor and headed to the hospital, thinking this might be the last time I'd see my son alive.

I never arrived; at least, a part of me didn't. In the car on the way, this Higher Being, this remote Power, this "unjust"

God, spoke to me through His Spirit. I felt His presence, soothing my still-hot anger. And I heard His voice, gentle, reassuring. He reminded me that I had made a commitment to Him, that I had promised to trust Him with my life, my all. And He had promised to take care of me, in all circumstances. "Take Me out of the box you've put Me in," He said, "and let Me work." By the time I parked the car, my heart was beating wildly. I sat for a few moments longer and uttered but two words in reply to all that had happened: "Forgive me."

By the time I reached Frank's room, I knew what I needed to do as clearly as if someone had given me written instructions. There had been no change in Frank's condition, so I sent Janice home to get some rest. Then I walked over to Frank's bed. Placing shaking hands on where I thought his kidneys should be, I prayed as I never believed I would ever pray. "God, forgive me for my ego, for trying to make You what I want You to be. If You will, heal my son, and if You won't, that's all right too. I'll trust You. But, please, do either right now, I pray in Christ's name. Amen."

That was all. There were no lightning flashes, no glowing

lights, no surges of emotion like the rushing wind, only the blip-blip-blip of monitors. I calmly sat down in a chair, picked up a magazine, and began to wait for God's answer. There was only one difference. For the first time in my life, I knew I was going to get one.

Within moments my eyes were drawn from the magazine to a catheter tube leading from Frank's frail-looking body. That tube was supposed to drain fluid from his kidneys, but for nearly two days it had been perfectly dry, meaning Frank's kidneys weren't working at all. But when I looked closely at the top of the tube, I saw a small drop of clear fluid forming. Ever so slowly it expanded, like a drop of water forming on the head of a leaky faucet, until it became heavy enough to run down the tube and into the collecting jar.

This was the most wonderful thing I had ever seen—the hand of God, working. I watched the tube, transfixed, fully expecting to see another drop of fluid form. In about two minutes, I did. Soon, the drops were coming regularly, about a minute apart. With every drip, I could hear God saying to me, "I am, and I care."

When the nurse came in on her regular half-hour rounds, she could barely contain her excitement. "Do you see this, do you see this?" she shouted, pointing to the collecting jar. "Do you know that this is more fluid than your son has excreted in the past forty-eight hours combined?" She grabbed the catheter and raised it, saying she wanted to get every drop, then rushed off.

Within minutes she was back. Grabbing a chair, she sat down next to me and, excitedly, we watched drops of fluid run down the tube. We were both awed at what was happening; for half an hour we murmured only short sentences. "Isn't God good?" she asked me once, and I nodded. When she finally got up to call the doctor, I went to call Janice.

An hour and a half later one of the specialists assigned to Frank's case arrived. Taking one look at the collector, he told us that it was a false alarm, that the fluid was too clear. Anything coming from a kidney as infected as Frank's was would be rust-colored and filled with pus. No, he said, the fluid had to be coming from somewhere else. But I knew—Frank was well again.

By the next morning more than five hundred centimeters of the clear fluid had passed into the collector, and it continued as the doctors ran tests and x-rays to try to determine its origin. Finally, two days later, our doctor called us into his office.

"Joe, Janice, I think we've been privileged to witness an act of God. All the x-rays taken in the last two days not only show no kidney infection, they show no sign that there was ever an infection. Frank's blood pressure and blood poison levels have also dropped suddenly. It is a definite miracle."

And this time I wasn't about to argue. At last I fully believed in a God whose love knows no bounds—not the bounds of logic, not the hold of natural laws. Faith. That's what I now had . . . that and the knowledge that one's belief in God is essentially hollow if the belief isn't founded on faith.

THUNDERSTRUCK

CHERIE HERRERA, LAKELAND, FLORIDA

Living in Fiji, I couldn't argue with the superlatives used to describe the South Pacific jewel where my parents were missionaries. What seventeen-year-old wouldn't be awed by the beauty of the crystal-clear water, the lushness of the palm trees and sugarcane fields, the fragrance of the soft tropical breezes?

Then came the beginning of the long wet season in November. The daily soaking rains wore on my nerves. Worse, though, was the violence of the tropical gales that could strike the islands at any time. The sound of the rain pounding on the tin roof was deafening and our wooden house shuddered.

One afternoon, about three o'clock, lightning flashed and thunder crashed. Still, I kept washing the lunch dishes.

I was determined not to let the storm get to me. Then something unexplainable came over me. Stop. Get away. I had to step back from the sink.

Just then there was a thunderclap so loud it drowned out my terrified scream. All the light bulbs in the house exploded and the microwave blew up. The air reeked of acrid smoke.

The storm over, Dad went outside to inspect the house. The roof was fine, but our water tank was damaged. Lightning had hit it, sending electric current through our pipes and wires. I remembered my fear and how I stepped suddenly away from the sink.

The very next day my grandmother phoned me from back home in Cincinnati.

"Are you all okay?" she asked. "My friend Donna called. She was upset. She woke up at ten o'clock at night with a terrible sense that you were in danger. She had an overwhelming urge to pray for you."

Ten? That would've been around three in the afternoon in Fiji, right after lunch, when the storm hit. Just before Grandma hung up, she said, "Oh, there's one more thing. Donna prayed specifically. Over and over she felt compelled to pray, 'Don't put your hands in the water.'"

Half a world away, I had gotten the warning.

The roiling contents burst out of the pot,
scalding Mom's chest and face.

5

HEALING SORROW

BERNADETTE MURCKO SANTANA, BROOKLYN, NEW YORK

Some seniors from church are going to the Holy Land, and I've decided to join them," my mother announced one evening. My brothers and sisters and I were relieved. We'd been worried Mom might never get over losing Dad. Her joy in life had gone out of her since he died. Even though she went to church daily, she seemed lonely and lost, as if her sorrow were too deep for anyone or anything to touch.

For years, my parents had talked about visiting the places they'd read about in the Bible, so I hoped this trip would help Mom feel connected to her faith again. Please, Lord, I asked, heal my mother.

One day a few weeks before she was set to leave, Mom was making stew when the top of the pressure cooker blew off. The roiling contents burst out of the pot, scalding Mom's chest and face. Fortunately, her burns healed in time for the trip.

"You're lucky," the doctor told her. "The only permanent damage you've suffered is to your tear ducts." They'd been destroyed and would never produce tears again, so Mom would have to use special eyedrops—artificial tears—for the rest of her life. Still, she was grateful her injuries wouldn't keep her from her long-awaited visit to the Holy Land.

Mom called as soon as she got back from her trip. I almost didn't recognize her voice because she sounded so happy. "Bernie," she said, "you won't believe what happened to me at the Garden of Gethsemane. I was wandering among the olive trees and rows of flowers, missing your dad so badly. At the rock where Jesus prayed before he went to the cross, I knelt and closed my eyes. I asked our Lord to forgive me for complaining about my own suffering when He had endured so much more.

"Then I felt this tickling sensation on my face. I opened my eyes, but nothing—not a leaf or flower petal—was brushing my skin. I reached up and touched my cheeks. They were wet, Bernie—wet with real tears!"

And so were mine.

153

154

WHERE TWO ARE GATHERED

JENNIFER BOLIN, POWDER SPRINGS, GEORGIA

The ringing phone woke me up. It was my friend Theresa, whose premature baby had been in the hospital for two months with a life-threatening infection. Little Bonnie had been doing well, so Theresa and her husband, Steve, were spending some much needed time at home.

Now Theresa was on the verge of panic: "The doctor called. Bonnie's heart keeps stopping. Can we pray together?"

I took a deep breath. "Lord, take our hands as we pray for Bonnie. We know your promise: Where two are gathered in Your name, You are there."

On the other end a gentle male voice joined in, his quiet, steady words mingling with mine. I had seen Steve at the hospital, his head bowed over the incubator while trying to will strength into his tiny daughter. As I prayed, I couldn't hear Theresa, only Steve, speaking with me almost in sync. It was as if he knew what I was going to say before my mouth shaped the words.

When we finished—together, precisely—I said, "Theresa, grab Steve's hand."

"Steve's not here," she said. "I'll call you from the hospital."

"Then who—?" I started to ask, but she had hung up. The next day, Theresa reported the infection had disappeared overnight. The baby was going to be okay.

"But who was on the line with us last night?" I asked Theresa, puzzled.

"Nobody. Steve was out on repair calls. You and I prayed alone."

No, I thought. Where two are gathered in His name . . .

"I've never seen a recovery from this much damage to a child's spinal cord."

THIRTY-FOUR HOURS TO SAVE MY SON

STEPHEN LORD, ENCINITAS, CALIFORNIA

My wife, Michele, and I stood staring through the plate-glass window into the intensive care unit of Children's Hospital-San Diego at our son. Nine-year-old Robert had been swinging on a dead acacia tree in our backyard when the tree toppled and his head hit the ground hard. Doctors suspected he'd broken his neck.

Michele and I and our five other children had rallied around Robert in the hospital that Sunday afternoon, March 15, 1998, assuring him he was going to be okay. But the doctor warned us otherwise.

"I've never seen a recovery from this much damage to a child's spinal cord," said Dr. Hal Meltzer, a pediatric neurosurgeon. He stood behind us as we watched our son, lying absolutely still, his head immobilized in a metal "halo." Michele was remarkably calm as she reached for my hand, but my knees felt weak, and my mind raced with questions: Will Robert be a quadriplegic? Will he ever walk again?

"Don't let anyone tell Robert he isn't going to get better," Michele told the doctor. "A lot of people are praying for him. A lot." She was resolute. Maybe it was her faith in God, which was something I did not share. Instead I thought: We have to face it—you don't recover from a broken neck.

Leaving Michele to stay with Robert at the hospital, I took the other children home. After putting them to bed, I tossed and turned, trying to think of something—anything—I could do to help our son. I'm a chemical engineer and head my own consulting firm. I approach everything logically. Facts are what I deal with. And the facts said that Robert faced lifelong paralysis.

By morning I'd come up with some ideas. Hoping that publicity might attract the attention of someone with vital information, I contacted a local TV station. Then I tried to get some work done until it was time to meet again with the surgeons at the hospital. But the prognosis was even more grim.

"There's always a chance for a miracle, of course," Dr. Meltzer said. "But I need to be honest with you. X-rays show your son's neck has been broken in several places. The vertebrae have been separated and the spinal cord is severely damaged. We should operate soon to prevent further damage." He paused. "If all goes well, he should be able to . . . to feed himself by fall."

To feed himself? Was that the most we could hope for? I must have groaned, because Michele put her hand on my arm. "Can't we wait," she asked, "to see if the swelling goes down and his neck begins to heal on its own?"

Dr. Meltzer shook his head. "Healing can't begin until Robert's neck is stabilized surgically," he said. But he did agree to postpone the operation for a few days. Meanwhile our son would continue to be treated with methylprednisolone, a steroid drug used for spinal cord injuries, and his head would remain immobilized in the halo.

Even though my intellect told me there was no practical way to help my son, my heart wanted him to get well. It wasn't logical, but I had to proceed as though it didn't matter what the doctors said. I wondered: Have we really heard all the options? Maybe there's something we could try that Robert's doctors haven't suggested. How can I find out? Whom can I call?

I went home desperate, then called a medical researcher I knew who worked at the Mayo Clinic; he was the father of one of my children's classmates. "I don't know anything about spinal cord injuries," he said. "But why don't you look on the Web?"

The Web. Although I work a lot on the computer, I wasn't that familiar with the World Wide Web, which provides vast sources of information via the Internet. But now it was time for me to plunge in. I sat down and typed "spinal cord injury" in the search box. In seconds a list of relevant websites and articles appeared on the screen.

For hours I read through studies, articles, and page after

page about conditions associated with paralysis, from brittle bones to heart disease. I can't let this happen to Robert!

I put my head in my hands and cried. Then I spotted a link for a website called Cure Paralysis Now. Cure? A spark of hope ignited within me. There, posted among scientific research papers, was an essay written by a twelfth-grade student. I almost skimmed right over it, but something made me go back and read carefully. In it was the mention of an experimental drug called GM-1 ganglioside. When given to an accident victim over a period of months, it had shown promise in reversing paralysis! But there was a condition for its use, and it was critical. Treatment had to begin within seventy-two hours of the injury.

Seventy-two hours! I looked at my watch—it was nearly 3:00 A.M. on Tuesday. It had been thirty-eight hours since Robert's accident. That left thirty-four hours—less than a day and a half—to find and get the drug. I wrote down the name of its principal researcher, Dr. Fred H. Geisler.

I couldn't get Dr. Geisler's number from information on the Web, so I called a Web-savvy associate, who found it in fifteen minutes on her computer at home.

At 8:00 A.M. I called his office and his secretary answered. "Dr. Geisler is out of town," she said. "Can I help?"

"I'm desperate," I said, explaining Robert's situation. "I need that drug out here by one o'clock tomorrow afternoon—Wednesday."

Quickly she gave me the name Fidia Pharmaceuticals, a Washington, D.C., company that is testing Sygen, the brand name for GM-1 ganglioside. I dialed frantically, leaving a series of messages until at last I reached someone authorized to deal with my situation. "Since this drug is experimental," she told me, "you'll need an okay from the Food and Drug Administration, which sometimes gives special dispensation for 'compassionate use.' I'll fax you the forms your physician needs to complete." Within minutes I was on my way to Dr. Meltzer's office with the forms. He was all for trying this.

At 4:00 P.M. Dr. Meltzer telephoned me to say he had received all the necessary approvals. But there was another hitch. By then it was seven o'clock in Washington. We'd missed Fidia's last air shipment and the company's next shipment to the West Coast wasn't until Thursday. I tried to stay calm, then remembered the delivery service operated by many airlines. "I'll get the stuff here, I promise," I told Dr. Meltzer.

I phoned a friend in Washington. Early Wednesday morning his wife picked up a month's supply of Sygen and rushed it to Dulles Airport. The package was put on a flight to Chicago, where it would be transferred to a connecting flight scheduled to arrive in San Diego at 1:00 P.M., exactly seventy-two hours after Robert's accident.

I called Michele at the hospital. "The drug is on its way," I said. But when I arrived with a TV camera crew at the baggage claim, the supervisor shook his head. "Big snowstorm in Chicago," he said. "Your package didn't make the connecting flight." When was the next flight in? "Seven o'clock tonight."

Six hours past the deadline for Robert! So close and yet . . . I felt like screaming in frustration. Then I thought of Michele's steadfast calm and her quiet belief. I have to trust that my boy will be all right.

When the package finally arrived shortly after seven o'clock, I signed for it and ran to my car. Fifteen minutes later I sprinted into the Children's Hospital ICU. As a nurse prepared the IV,

Michele and I stood by, arms around each other. Within minutes the drug was flowing into Robert's system.

The following afternoon Robert shifted his right arm slightly. Over the next few days he was able to move the arm more and more. Gradually, feeling returned to his right side, then his left. An operation was performed to help stabilize the area and he began physical therapy. By the end of May, Robert was out of the hospital, still wearing the halo but able to move on his own with the aid of a walker.

When he returned to school in September, the halo had been removed and even the walker was relegated to a corner of his room. Today Robert walks with a slight limp and continues to receive physical therapy, but he's doing fine and is keeping up with his schoolwork.

"Thank you, Lord," Michele said one day as she watched Robert kicking a soccer ball around. Yes, even I have to agree. The drug might have been effective even past the seventy-two-hour deadline; but when I look back over everything that happened, I know something else was at work.

All those prayers, by Michele and so many others, had to

have been effective too. During those three days I found myself operating from a place I had never been before—living for possibilities instead of facing up to supposed facts. I'd experienced a leap of faith.

I still have a long way to go, but one Sunday soon after Robert came home from the hospital, I went to church. And there I did something new for me. I said a prayer and thanked God. It seemed the logical thing to do.

A DOCTOR'S BOLDNESS

STONEY ABERCROMBIE, M.D., GREENWOOD, SOUTH CAROLINA

The tropical sun beat mercilessly on Yulansoni, a village of mud-brick huts in Tanzania, East Africa, on August 21, 1996. Ten years earlier I had started Volunteers in Medical Missions (VIMM), which now serves poverty-stricken people in seventeen countries throughout the world. None were more needy than the hundreds of multi-tribed villagers who stood before us. A few wore nothing but grass skirts, their earlobes cut according to custom. The bush landscape around us concealed lions, gazelles, monkeys, and occasional bandits.

Our team consisted of six doctors, two nurses, two premed students, eight local translators, the local Christian missionary, and our bus driver. That day, before beginning our clinic work, I told the story of the Israelites crossing the Red Sea as they fled from the Egyptians. They were saved not by their own power, I explained to the crowd, but by relying on God, who held the waters aside for them so they could cross on dry land.

Midafternoon, as we were working in the hut built for our use as a clinic, people from a village five miles distant carried in a woman too weak to walk. Burning with fever, dehydrated, her black skin paled, she lay on the table unable to sit up and in obvious pain. The extreme whiteness of her eyes indicated anemia; the distension and rigidity of her abdomen indicated internal bleeding and infection. A few questions and answers led us to diagnose a ruptured tubal pregnancy.

Under the best conditions in a modern hospital, her chance of survival might have been 50 percent, and survival would bring complications. But the nearest hospital was 300 kilometers away.

She was given two liters of intravenous fluid and an injection of antibiotics. There was nothing more we could do for her medically. My clinical judgment told me she would die that night, if not within the next few hours.

I asked the native missionary to speak to her in Swahili for me. "Do you know Jesus Christ as your saviour?" I asked.

"I've never heard of Him," came back the feeble reply.

"May I tell you about Him?"

"Yes."

Believe me, I do not usually have such conversations with my patients. Yet I felt an urge to prepare the woman for death. I explained briefly how Jesus came from heaven to love everyone, and how when people die they will go to heaven if they believe He is the Son of God.

Through the interpreter I said a prayer that the woman repeated after me: "Please forgive me for anything wrong I have done. I want to live with You in heaven. I realize who You are and I want to be a part of You."

Then an unaccustomed boldness came upon me. Why couldn't we believe God could heal her? In the Bible such things happened. Of course, it might not be God's will to heal her, I reasoned, but if it were, what a wonderful way to show the Yulansoni villagers the power of God!

Aloud, through the interpreter and before those present, I asked in prayer that if it were God's will, He would heal her.

I'm not sure what I expected to see when I opened my eyes. Unlike people in Bible stories, the woman did not get up from the table and walk. Instead, she continued to lie there helplessly. As tears of compassion rolled down my face, I could only feel I had done what I could to prepare her for death.

Since the friends who had brought the woman had since returned to their village, we lifted her into our bus and took her to her village, laying her gently on the dirt floor of her mud hut. We told her drunken husband that his wife was very ill and might die, but he received our interpreted message with an equanimity attributable, I thought, either to his state of intoxication or to the low value their culture places on women.

As I sat in the back of the bus on the way to our home base in Singida, I quietly communed with God. "Lord," I prayed, "for Your glory, please cure this woman." Gradually I became infused with an inner peace that told me God was indeed going to heal her. Rising from my seat, I said to the other team members, "I feel in my heart that the woman has been healed!"

Silence. *He's really put his foot in his mouth this time,* I imagined them thinking. Maybe I had. Who was I to think God would perform a miracle just because I had prayed for it?

The next day, we returned to Yulansoni and I asked for news of the woman. Had she died? But since her village lay five miles distant, no one knew. Wednesday, our last day in Yulansoni, I asked again. Still no one had any news. If she had died, the missionary informed me, she would already have been buried, for tropical conditions mandated rapid interment.

Usually mission clinics are noisy. Crowds mill; children cry; doctors, patients, and interpreters talk simultaneously. So I felt curiosity and some alarm at midafternoon when a sudden hush interrupted my patient examination. I looked up to see the crowd of people parting like the Red Sea to let a barefoot woman in a handmade, pullover dress pass through.

Afraid to believe, I found myself walking over and putting my arm around her. Through the interpreter I asked, "Are you all right?" Her smile answered me more eloquently than words. She told us she had walked the five miles from her village—with no pain or discomfort. I gave her a thorough examination. Her abdomen had returned to normal. She had no fever. Her healing was complete.

In an awed whisper, one of my colleagues asked, "Our medicines didn't heal her, did they? It was the prayer and a miracle, wasn't it?"

"Yes," I replied, "it was."

The primary directive of Volunteers in Medical Missions indicates that teams must make a difference in the lives of those they visit. This year we are returning to Yulansoni to build a combination medical clinic and church to care for both the physical and spiritual needs of the villagers. We expect to make a difference in their lives—and we are glad to know that once in a while God steps in and makes the difference by Himself.

I awoke in the hospital with both legs and an arm broken, third-degree burns over 20 percent of my body, and a severe head injury.

7

WINDOWS

Pamela Kay Barnett, Imlay City, Michigan

I was twenty years old, newly married, and making the long drive to Camp Pendleton to visit my husband, Jimmy, who was stationed there for infantry training. As I crested a hill on the two-lane highway, a car came straight at me. I later learned a drunk driver, trying to pass six cars on a blind hill, had hit me head-on, causing my car to spin around. Then I got hit again, and the gas tank exploded.

I awoke in the hospital with both legs and an arm broken,

third-degree burns over 20 percent of my body, and a severe head injury. My left ear had been burned away and one hand was so badly mangled that it might have to be removed. Doctors had little hope for my survival. My family came from all around the country, expecting a funeral. When my condition stabilized, one by one they had to return to their homes and jobs.

About a month after the accident, Jimmy, who had been by my side every day, also had to leave. I was still in intensive care, in traction, and the damage to my eyes meant I could only see shadow and light. Recovery would be a long and painful process, especially without Jimmy there. "This is too much to bear," I cried out to God one day. "Please let me know that you are here. I have never felt so alone in my life."

Almost instantly I noticed a bright sunbeam sweeping across the sheets next to my face. It seemed to quiver with energy and radiate peace and reassurance. The light remained with me all that day. It was a simple thing, a light from a window, but it gave me comfort.

After I was released from the hospital, I told Jimmy the story of how that ray of sunlight had consoled me during the time he couldn't be with me. When I finished, he had a puzzled look on his face. "Pam, you were in intensive care," he said quietly. "There were no windows."

VISIONS
OF ANGELS

For he shall give his angels charge over thee.

to keep thee in all thy ways.

A SAFE RIDE

CAROLINE CAMPBELL

I love riding my bike—whizzing around my neighborhood, pedaling down to Point Park with my sister. I'm a good rider and never have accidents. Well, almost never.

It was a sunny Sunday, and I was out riding my bike. I did not have my helmet on. Most of the time I didn't bother wearing it around my neighborhood. After all, what could happen there? But as I was circling around in my driveway, I heard a voice call my name. "Caroline," the voice said. "Put on your helmet."

I looked all around, but no one was there. The voice had been sweet and soft, so I wasn't scared. I hopped off my bike and went inside to get my helmet.

About an hour later, I was riding home from the park when my tire slipped off the paved road. I was going kind of fast, and my bike wobbled, then skidded, and . . . BOOM! I flew over my handlebars and landed on my head.

My sister, who was riding behind me, raced home and got my dad. When he got there, I was sitting beside my bike, running my fingers over a huge dent in the front of my helmet. A dent that could have been in my forehead!

I've never again heard that voice, but I believe it was an angel from God, helping to keep me safe. I believe whenever I ride my bike, an angel is with me. And, if angels smile, I'm sure that one is grinning down at the top of my helmet—which I now wear everywhere!

I was once again in intensive care, hooked up to oxygen and a slew of beeping, blinking monitors.

ON THE BRINK OF HEAVEN

Bethany Withrow, Roanoke, Virginia

All night the pounding of my heart kept me drifting in and out of sleep. Now, on a frosty December morning in 1994, I pulled myself from underneath the warm blankets with great difficulty. Every day, it seemed, I awakened more exhausted than the day before.

Eight years earlier, at seventeen, I had been diagnosed with lupus erythematosus, a degenerative systemic condition that produces a range of debilitating, sometimes mysterious symptoms, including arthritis. For months I had been battling a severe flare-up that had kept me prisoner in my house—except for stays in the hospital when I had fever as high as 106 degrees. As a result of steroid drugs, I developed diabetes. Today I felt worse than I had in months.

Even breathing was painful. But something stranger was happening. When I touched my face, it felt unusual. I hobbled to the bathroom and sought my reflection in the mirror. Staring back at me was a face I hardly recognized. It was horribly swollen and my left eye drooped.

"Butch!" I called to my husband. He took one look at me and ran for the phone. "I'm calling the doctor."

Dr. Alexander told him to bring me right over. My husband had been by my side through many lupus crises, so to see him this unnerved scared me. I began to worry that I had suffered a stroke. Then in the living room, as I struggled with my coat, a flash of brown through the window caught my eye. There in our wooded yard stood a baby, white-tailed deer all alone. How strange he came this close, I thought. Our gazes met and lingered, and I began to feel calm. I love animals. Suddenly, with a graceful little jump, he was gone. But a small measure of that calmness stayed with me.

We were almost out the door when my mom called from Wichita, Kansas, to check on me. I could tell how worried she was. When I was little, Mom used to say she asked God for a "hedge of angels" to protect her children. I reminded her to ask God to keep His angels close to me today.

Lupus is a disease of many guises, and Dr. Alexander could not determine what was wrong with me or how to treat it. He took x-rays and drew blood, then sent me home to rest. "Keep still and call me immediately if you get worse, Beth," he said. I knew he was trying to spare me another traumatic hospital stay. Unless my condition was life threatening, I wanted to be at home.

In the car I studied Butch. I knew he hated leaving me to go in to work. He walked me inside the house and made sure I was comfortable on the couch. Then, as he leaned over to kiss me, I felt a tear fall on my brow. "Don't worry," I whispered. "I'm going to be all right."

But the symptoms worsened. I tossed and turned on the

couch, my heart thundering. Late in the day I finally tried calling Dr. Alexander but couldn't reach him. I was getting weaker. I talked to Mom again and she said she and her friends at church were praying for me for all they were worth. After we hung up, Mom was so worried she called my father, who lives nearby. He came over to check on me and wasted no time getting me to the hospital.

8

By midnight I was once again in intensive care, hooked up to oxygen and a slew of beeping, blinking monitors. Butch had taken up his familiar position in a recliner by my bed, while doctors and nurses paraded in and out of my room. Eventually, around 3:30 in the morning, the traffic slowed. Butch nodded off while holding my hand, and I thought I was falling asleep too. Then I realized something altogether different was happening to me, something both wondrous and fantastic.

I drifted in a smoky grayness, not quite floating and not quite walking. I was free of all the medical equipment I had been tethered to moments before. I traveled down an extended passageway. It felt like being inside a telescope; in the dim distance I discerned a glow. With amazement I realized I was no longer in pain. I moved effortlessly toward a radiant, golden light. As I drew closer, I noticed a beautiful figure within the light, standing with outstretched arms. Indescribable peace flooded my senses; the feeling expanded the closer I came to the figure emanating from the light.

All at once I knew I was in the presence of the Son of God. Angels were everywhere, flying to and fro as they hastened to do the Lord's work, each encircled in its own golden bubble of light. Their flowing gowns were translucent and their features were serene, noble and wise.

I was aware of Jesus communicating directly with me, though no words were uttered. His language flowed through me. He told me not to be afraid, that he wasn't ready for me yet, that I would be going back: *There are still things for you to do and songs for you to sing.* An overpowering sensation of being loved seized me. I felt a joy I had never felt before—the full experience of Christ's love for me.

Suddenly, as if a curtain had been drawn back, I found myself amidst breathtaking surroundings: magnificent mountains, rolling pastures, and singing brooks. I saw a distant red barn and I was happy because I knew this meant there were animals in heaven. I thought of the baby deer I had seen that morning and all the animals I loved.

I noticed a couple standing behind Jesus, and angels hovering and singing above them. I recognized my grandmother, who, before she died the previous year, had been doubled over with osteoporosis. Now she stood straight and tall, holding the hand of my granddaddy. He died long before I was born but I had seen many pictures of him. In his free hand he held a bowl. I knew what it contained. Mama loved to tell about her daddy's prowess in the kitchen.

Saturdays were special. That's when Granddaddy reveled in making his special chili, full of secret, savory ingredients. That bowl contained Granddaddy's Saturday-night chili. And far from seeming irrelevant or bizarre, this fantastic detail reassured me that my grandparents were happy, together again in their love, and that heaven was a place God has made for each of us.

Then Jesus was communicating with me again. "I have given you a special husband, and I have given him strength so he can care for you." I was always aware that Butch was unique;

now the words of Jesus filled me with pride and gratitude.

He reminded me once more that there was much left for me to do; then I was zooming backwards through the telescopic passageway as if time had been reversed. Almost instantly I was in my hospital bed again, reattached to the monitors and oxygen. But I was not disappointed. I was thankful and brimming with joy.

Immediately I wanted to tell Butch all about my amazing experience, but he was sleeping so peacefully, I did not have the heart to disturb him. I wondered why the monitors hadn't sounded an alarm while I was gone. My journey had seemed to last a long while. God's time, though, is different; what feels to us like hours may be only a blink of the eye in heaven.

For the first time since returning, I looked around the room, and there they were: angels, angels everywhere, flickering like candlelight, hovering protectively around us like a hedge—a hedge of angels.

No one sleeps late in the hospital. Soon the nurses and doctors were busy, and Butch woke up. I told him all about my experience and he listened intently, stroking my hand, never doubting for a moment that what had happened to me was real.

All that day things looked markedly different, as if a bit of the light I had seen now touched and infused everyone and everything I encountered. I continued to sense the presence of heavenly beings in my room. Even Butch seemed to have an angelic glow about him.

The doctors were amazed to see that the swelling in my face had gone down and the position of my eye was back to normal. They continued running tests for the next few days, including an MRI. When they slipped me into the cylinder for that test, it was like being back in the heavenly passageway, and again I saw the angels. In the waiting room before the test, a frightened little boy was waiting his turn. I saw an angel hovering over him. I told him what I saw, and he became calm.

At last Dr. Alexander said I could go home. "All we know, Beth," he reported, "is that you suffered a major lupus flare-up and now you're getting better. But you were very, very sick." Then, smiling, he said, "Don't scare me like that again!"

I don't want to scare anybody because I know from my journey that there is nothing to fear when we are with God. He protects us and loves us at all times. Full awareness of that love is the greatest healer of all.

Nothing about life has been the same for me since I saw the angels. I no longer have to take insulin; my fever is gone; my heart beats normally. I still have lupus and I get sick, but it is not as bad or as terrifying as before. Now I have a continual sense of life's secret beauty.

I finally sat down and told Mom the whole story, and she cried tears of elation that her parents were happy with God, and that a hedge of angels protected her daughter.

A FATHER'S MESSAGE

CATHY SLACK, GLENDALE, ARIZONA, AS TOLD TO SKIP WESTPHAL

S tay away from the pool, Danny," I told my three-year-old as he headed for the backyard to ride his Big Wheel.

"Yes, Mom," he said obediently.

Listening to the sound of his plastic tricycle, I returned to the kitchen, sighing. It was not easy being a widow, and raising two children on my own was often a strain. I busied myself about the house until something made me stop dead still. I cocked my ear. No sounds of Danny's tricycle. I rushed to the window and looked out at the swimming pool. Danny's Big Wheel was bobbing in the water, and there, floating face down, was Danny.

Desperately I pulled Danny out of the water and tried to administer CPR, but his body was cold and his face was gray. Then came the sirens, the paramedics, the helicopter whisking Danny off to the hospital, where he lay in a coma. Finally, after my long, prayerful vigil, Danny opened his eyes. Soon he was well again, back home playing as usual. But somehow he seemed changed.

One day he blurted out, "Mom, I want to see a picture of my daddy." I had not realized I had never shown him a picture of his father, who had died before Danny was born. The first photograph I brought out showed my husband and his baseball team.

Danny looked at it for a few moments. Then he pointed to one of the coaches. "That's my daddy," he said.

"How do you know?" I asked.

"He talked to me in the hospital before I woke up. He said, 'You must go home now. Mommy needs you.'"

I looked at the man he'd pointed to; it was the father he had never seen.

What in life is more realistic than faith,
more practical, really, than hope?

189

Easter Awakening

Delores Bates, Toledo, Ohio

I leaned over the hospital bed in which my eighteen-year-old son, Art, lay in a comatose state that seemed like death. He was being fed through tubes; a machine breathed for him, breaking the harsh stillness of the room with mechanical gasps. I moved close to Art's ear and whispered, "Honey, I had a dream last night, so beautiful that it seemed real. Two magnificent angels stood by your bed. It means you will be healed, I know it."

Did he hear me? Can the soul hear when the body is asleep? Art didn't move, didn't acknowledge my words. If only he would open his eyes! Just that, Lord.

Before the accident two nights earlier, this limp form under the stiff hospital bedsheets had been a strapping high school senior, star captain of his football team, and the finest son a mother could ever want. Proud of the body God had given him, Art did not drink or smoke. He held strong values and went to church regularly. His dream was to play professional football and set a good example for other young people.

But now doctors held out little hope that he would walk or talk or do anything productive again. It was as if Art had gone on and left his broken body behind. Could that be true?

On the evening of January 1, 1989, Art had attended a dance with some friends. When his father and I went to bed that night, a cold rain beat at the windows. I am usually a sound sleeper, but at about 1:00 A.M. I awoke with a start and shook my husband. "Arthur," I said, my heart racing, "I'm afraid something terrible has happened to our boy." Before I could get back to sleep, a call came from St. Vincent's Hospital. Art had been driving his friends home when a pickup truck turned into the side of his car, slamming it into a tree. One of Art's passengers died. The others weren't badly hurt. But Art lay close to death in the emergency room.

I will never forget the panic of that night, the dread and the sense of helplessness as my boy fought for life. After Arthur and I threw on some clothes, we raced in our car to St. Vincent's. Along with some friends and family members we had alerted, we huddled together and prayed unceasingly while doctors frantically worked on Art. The news from the operating room was grim; Art's windpipe and chest were nearly crushed from the impact with the steering wheel. Most worrisome was the injury to his brain.

9

"All that's saved him so far," one doctor told us, "is his strong athlete's body. But the area around his brain stem is so severely damaged he might never regain consciousness."

At about 5:00 A.M. Dr. Frank A. Redmond finally came to us and said Art's condition was stabilized and he would be moved into the intensive care unit. He revealed that on at least one occasion that night Art had been clinically dead but they were able to revive him. "I did a lot of praying," Dr. Redmond admitted. "Something kept your boy alive."

Eventually they let us see Art in ICU. I tiptoed to his bedside. To see him so still, to see the breathing tube in his trachea, his closed and swollen eyes—my own flesh and blood—it was devastating. I collapsed into my husband's arms and sobbed inconsolably. "We can't give up," he whispered, holding me tight. "We have to keep praying for a miracle."

I wiped my eyes and turned back to Art. Would his eyes ever open again, his lips speak, or his arms move voluntarily? Would he ever again sneak up behind me in the kitchen, throw those muscled arms around my waist, and kiss me, saying, "Ma, I sure do love ya"?

The doctors didn't think so. "Even if he does wake up," said one, "he probably won't be able to walk. He won't have a memory. He won't know who you are."

I refused to believe my own son wouldn't know me. God is merciful. Asleep in a nearby room the hospital let me use that night, I was given a different prognosis. In a dream as vivid as life, I saw two colossal angels floating over Art's bed, one above his head and the other at his side. They were glowing, shimmering, their streaming robes lighter than air. Their faces were indistinct, but they had a golden brilliance that emanated love, compassion, and healing. Then I saw Art sitting up in bed, talking with his friends. My heart beat with joy; my son would be healed! What else could this vision mean?

I awakened with the images still flowing through my mind and rushed into Art's room, half expecting to see him sitting up in bed laughing. But he was still in a coma, still near death. That is when I pressed my lips close and whispered my dream to him.

From then on I carried the picture of those two great heavenly beauties in my mind's eye, and every day I reminded Art about them. I knew his spirit heard me. That's why we talked to him—his father and I, our relatives and ministers, his friends from school, and the football team and his coaches. We talked to Art constantly, telling him how much we loved him, keeping a vigil.

Thirty days passed. I was at my son's side continually, talking, praying, playing tapes from friends. I refused to believe he wouldn't get up out of that bed, that he wouldn't know me. The doctors tried to temper my optimism, while we continued to pray.

What in life is more realistic than faith, more practical, really, than hope? Isn't that all I had? I knew my son would get well. I kept visualizing it and thanking the Lord, over and over again.

But it was hard to keep believing as the weeks wore on—to see my boy fed by tubes when he used to feast on my cooking, my homemade lasagna and fried chicken.

Finally Art was transferred to St. Francis Hospital in Green Springs. Every time I came to visit him the nurses would shake their heads, knowing the question that was on my lips: Has there been a change? Anything?

Three months passed. Then I saw the angels again.

It was during Holy Week, and Art's older sister, Rachael, and I had been talking about how much Art loved Easter. Again one night I dreamed I was at Art's bedside. Those same golden angels, seemingly both powerful and compassionate, looked over my son, who was awake, his eyes alert and bright. This time, however, the angels were both on Art's right. I took this as a reaffirmation of God's message.

Art's eyes opened on Good Friday. I had had a special feeling when I came to see him that afternoon. When I walked into his room those big, brown eyes were looking right at me. Could it really be? I slowly walked around the bed. Art's eyes followed. He was awake! He was tracking me! I fell to my knees at his bedside and gave thanks.

Doctors, however, were cautious about interpreting this too optimistically. Then came Easter. As his father and I arrived for a visit after church, a nurse rushed up waving a piece of paper. In a handwriting I knew as well as my own was our phone number, obviously written out with great difficulty. "It was as if he wanted us to call you," the nurse reported. "His memory is intact!" On the day of our Saviour's resurrection, part of Art had been resurrected too. He hadn't forgotten us.

A month went by and nothing much changed. Art still had not uttered a word since coming out of his coma. One day Art's grandmother accompanied me to the hospital. When we left Art's room, she lamented, "Delores, I don't think he's ever going to talk again!"

I was about to respectfully disagree when a familiar voice jolted us: "Ma!"

We froze. It rang out again, loud and clear. "Ma!"

Art was talking. His first word now was the first word he had ever said as a baby: Ma. I knew the Lord would not let my son forget his mother.

Though his words were few and hesitant, the hospital immediately began speech therapy, followed quickly by physical therapy. His progress was slow initially until a therapist used a little psychology and a mirror. The athlete in Art was proud of the body he had taken care of so well. When the therapist showed Art how his physique had atrophied during the coma, Art's face tightened over with determination. From then on he strove tirelessly to regain his old physical form.

Finally Art was able to tell us what he recalled about the night of the accident. "I remember being on the operating table," he said. "I saw the doctors working. Three times I tried to leave my body and three times the Holy Spirit made me go back because my family was praying and God would heal me."

Art has had a long road back, and I still remind him about the angels I saw in my dream whenever his struggle is wearing him down. That always seems to pick him up. His speech was slow for a long time, but now he speaks almost as well as he did before the accident. He walks with a cane, but leans on it less and less. This June he will graduate from the University of Toledo with a degree in marketing. Art still wants to play football again someday, which some people might think is too optimistic. But Art believes that with the power of many prayers behind him, anything is possible.

I know it's a miracle when my son sneaks up behind me in the kitchen, slips his arms around my waist, kisses me, and says, "Ma, I sure do love ya." It's the miracle we prayed for and the one the angels in my dream promised. It's the miracle of my Art, alive today.

A LIGHTED CROSS

BILL DOLACK, WOODSVILLE, NEW HAMPSHIRE

My dad was in the hospital battling an intestinal infection when his vital signs plummeted and he was rushed to the operating room. After a hurried consultation with Dad's doctors, Mother braced my sister and me for the worst.

Throughout my childhood, my father had survived a number of serious medical problems, including a heart attack and cancer. He'd seen the four walls of a hospital room more times than anyone should have to. Lord, I prayed, no matter what, please comfort him.

Dad pulled through. As soon as he felt better, he told us something amazing about that day in the operating room.

"I was scared. I knew I was dying," he said. "I shifted my head to one side and watched the nurses prepping for the operation. Beyond them I saw a large window. Out in the dusk was a lighted cross, glowing as if meant for me. I stared out that window, my eyes focused on the brilliant outline. My fears subsided. Then the anesthesia took hold."

Dad recovered fully and several months later went to visit a friend at the same hospital. In the parking lot Dad looked around for the cross he'd seen through the window. He could not find it. Inside he ran into one of the nurses who had taken care of him. "Can I take a quick look at the operating room where I had my surgery?" he asked. The room was free so she took him in. My father was dumbfounded. There was no window in that room. All four walls were solid through and through.

*J awakened from my coma three weeks
after the fire to discover that J had
burns on 50 percent of my body.*

MEMORY OF FIRE

Lesia Cartelli, Encinitas, California

The instant I stepped inside the burning building, the old fear gripped me. Logically, I knew that there was no real danger—that the fire had been set on purpose as a training exercise, and that firefighters were positioned all around outside, ready to extinguish the blaze at a moment's notice. But that knowledge melted away to nothing as I watched the ink-black streams of smoke creep up the walls and felt the first terrible waves of heat against my skin. I dropped the fire hose I'd been carrying and ran out of the building.

My long, painful relationship with fire began on a Sunday visit to my grandmother's house in the suburbs of Detroit in 1969, when I was nine years old. There had been an odor of gas in the house for some days, but the men from Gas and Electric hadn't been able to find a leak. "You girls better go play down in the basement," Grandma told my five-year-old cousin Kimmie and me. "There's less of a smell down there." Little did my grandparents and the repairmen know, the gas leak was actually coming directly from underground.

Kimmie and I decided on hide-and-seek. I was it. I turned my face to a wall near the furnace, closed my eyes, and started counting while Kimmie ran and hid. "24...23...22...21...." Just as I got to three, the furnace exploded.

Smoke, falling debris, and flames were everywhere. Then, out of the chaos, a light appeared—a light that was different from the hot, red flames all around me. It was cool, blue, otherworldly. I staggered toward it. I found myself looking at a hole that the explosion had blown in the side of the house. My clothes and my hair were on fire. Screaming, I scrambled through the hole and out onto the lawn.

The trip to the hospital was a blur. The next thing I knew, I was floating above my hospital bed, totally at peace. Looking down, I saw my own body, wrapped in white bandages. I felt a huge swell of relief that I wasn't in that body anymore.

I glided up a long, wide flight of stairs. At the top, three angels were standing, bathed in the same blue light that had guided me out of the basement. I don't know exactly how we communicated, but the message they sent was clear. It wasn't my time yet. I would have to go back. But whenever things got bad, all I needed to do was close my eyes and think of them. They would always be nearby.

I awakened from my coma three weeks after the fire to discover that I had burns on 50 percent of my body. My face was terribly scarred. I underwent seventeen plastic surgeries. At school the other kids taunted me, called me a monster. In fifth grade, a teacher stood me up in front of the class as an example of why kids should never play with matches. My grandparents were consumed with guilt over what had happened. Kimmie escaped the accident with only minor injuries, but she moved away shortly after the fire. We never got to talk about it.

The physical scars weren't the only ones the fire left behind. As an adult I lived each and every day in fear. I had to force myself to fill my tank at the gas station. At the movies, I'd look away if a fire scene came on screen. The fear attacked me with the same merciless hunger that the flames themselves had.

Through all those years, the only thing that kept me going was the memory of my angels and the promise they'd made. Whenever things got really bad, I would stop what I was doing, close my eyes, and think of them. Remember, I would tell myself, whether I can see them or not, they're always right here with me. I held on to that promise with all my might.

When I was in my thirties, I got involved helping local kids who were burn victims. I knew these children suffered, like I did, from both inner and outer scars, and that it was often difficult for them to talk about how they felt. Because of what I'd been through, they opened up to me. I also started a summer camp exclusively for kids who'd suffered burns.

If I was going to tell these kids to open up and trust the

healing process, I had to do the same myself. Fear of fire still haunted me terribly. Somehow I, too, needed to face my fears.

I met a local fire chief and asked him if he knew of some way I might be able to do this.

"Fire is dangerous," he said. "Your fear and respect are well founded. Don't try to change that." For a while I gave up on the idea. Then one day my work with young burn victims happened to take me to a firefighters' conference in San Jose, California.

That's where I met Bruce. He was a training officer for the San Diego Fire Department. He knew everything there was to know about fire from a fireman's perspective. But he was interested in learning more about how a fire victim felt. When I told him my story and about my idea of facing my fear, he was more than just encouraging. He was ready to help me do it.

"I supervise training fires for my crew all the time," he said. "In fact, there's one coming up in just a few weeks. I'd like to bring you along."

The test building was a four-story tower on an isolated tarmac about half an hour inland from San Diego. On the drive there, my fears threatened again to overtake me. I almost turned back, but I gripped the wheel tight and just tried to think of my angels. At the test site Bruce outfitted me in full firefighter's gear and showed me how to handle the hose. A fire was started in the building's basement. "Just keep reminding yourself it's a test," he said. "You're going to do just fine."

How I had wanted to "do just fine" too—for Bruce, for myself, for my angels. But when I reached that top step leading down to the basement and the flames, all the encouragement blew away in an instant. There was nothing left but that terrible, relentless fear. I couldn't go through with it.

Bruce caught up with me outside. "I'm sorry," I said. "I tried, I really did. But I just can't do it." There really was no way out—no escape for me, ever, from the prison of those memories.

Bruce put his arm around my shoulder. "We're going to do three more burns today. You've got three more chances, if you want them. It's up to you."

I sat out on that tarmac for an hour. Slowly I found myself letting go—of my expectations, of my anger, of my fear. I thought back again to the promise my angels had made so long ago. No matter what happened in my life, they would always be there. Always.

By the tower, Bruce was getting the firefighters prepared for the next exercise. I got to my feet and walked over. "Okay," I said. "I'm ready to try again."

Armed with my hose, I took one careful, steady step at a time toward the basement stairs. At the top step, the waves of hot, choking air again rolled up at me. But this time I went all the way down to the bottom.

That's when I saw them—bathed in that same blue light I saw long ago. My three angels. I trained my hose on the fire and sprayed. As the flames fell away, so did the fear that had gripped my heart for so many years.

Out on the tarmac I hugged Bruce as tears of joy streamed down my cheeks. I had made it through the flames and the fear at last. And my angels had been there, just as they'd promised.

AUTHOR INDEX

Abercrombie, Stoney, M.D., 165

Abruzzini, Anne, 41

Bates, Delores, 189

Barnett, Pamela Kay, 171

Bolin, Jennifer, 154

Campbell, Caroline, 176

Carney, Art, 113

Cartelli, Lesia, 200

Conklin, Elissa Hadley, 15

Creager, Freda, 131

Davis, Christopher, 126

Dolack, Bill, 198

Harvey, Billie F., 34

Hasapes, Helen, 53

Herrera, Cherie, 148

Lord, Stephen, 156

Ludolf, Marilyn, 68

Matthews, Dale A., M.D., 89

Maurer, Pearl, 38

McCusker, Sue, 49

Noble, Jan, 17

Paris, Joan B., 51

Perry, Amanda, 100

Potter, Cookie, 78

Renich-Meyers, Jill, 62

Rice, Janelle, 32

Robbins, Sally H., 111

Rogers, Carly Dawn, 22

Rudesill, Barry, 64

Santana, Bernadette Murcko, 151

Skillern, Christine, 26

Slack, Cathy, 187

Sowers, Laura Z., 10

Stevenson, Joe, 138

Vairin, Donald, 20

Wagster, Imogene, 98

Wakefield, Dan, 80

Whitley, Karen, 136

Wilford, Emma, 120

Withrow, Bethany, 178

Wood, Patricia Walworth, 24

Zier, Terry A., 43

TITLE INDEX

Book Lady, The, 43

Call Roy Stanley, 26

Calling the In-laws, 15

Changed Man, A, 113

Doctor's Boldness, A, 165

Easter Awakening, 189

Father's Message, A, 187

Flutter of Tiny Wings, The, 32

Full Recovery, A, 136

Granny's Wings, 78

Hailstorm of Healing, A, 111

Heal Me, O Lord, 68

Healing Effect, The, 89

Healing Sorrow, 151

Healing Touch, 100

Hearing Restored, 22

Help from a New Friend, 24

I Saw the Hand of God Move, 138

Journey on Good Friday, 131

Lighted Cross, A, 198

Memory of Fire, 200

Message from a Friend, 62

My Own Life Is Proof, 80

Not on the Menu, 98

On the Brink of Heaven, 178

Pacific Ocean Rescue, 20

Rescued from a Bee Sting, 38

Rise Up and Walk, 51

Safe Place, A, 126

Safe Ride, A, 176

Search for a Surgeon, 41

Someone at My Side, 64

Third Doctor, The, 49

Thirty-four Hours to Save My Son, 156

Thunderstruck, 148

Unexpected Garden, An, 34

Unlikely Meeting, An, 17

Visit to a Flower Shop, 53

Where Two Are Gathered, 154

While My Parents Slept, 120

Windows, 171

Woman from Nowhere, The, 10